9-94
13.00
B+T
VER

P9-DIB-155

HV   Hamilton, Arthur   18,229
9468
.H22 Father behind bars
A3
1993

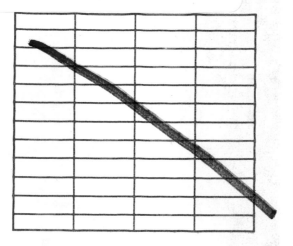

Father behind bars
HV9468.H22A3 93   18229

Hamilton, Arthur
        VRJC/WRIGHT LIBRARY

DEMCO

FATHER BEHIND BARS

FATHER BEHIND BARS

by Arthur Hamilton, Jr. and William Banks

WRS
PUBLISHING

A Division of WRS Group, Inc.
Waco, Texas

Text copyright © 1993 by Arthur Hamilton, Jr. and William Banks.

All rights reserved. No part of this book may be reproduced or transmitted in any form or by any means, electronic or mechanical, including photocopying or recording or by any information storage or retrieval system, without permission in writing from the publisher.

First published in the United States of America in 1993 by WRS Publishing, A Division of WRS Group, Inc., 701 N. New Road, Waco, Texas 76710
Book design by Kenneth Turbeville
Jacket design by Joe James

10 9 8 7 6 5 4 3 2

Library of Congress Catalog Card Number

ISBN 1-56796-034-0

Dedication

This book is dedicated to all souls suffering, in and out of prisons; to all victims of criminal acts committed against their persons; and to all African Americans striving to be somebody in a racist and seemingly insensitive nation.

Arthur's Acknowledgments

Special thanks to Donald Goines and Alice Walker for showing me, through their accomplishments, that I could dream and that I can make my dreams come true.

Very special thanks to my wife, Marilyn, and all five of our wonderful children for giving me all the support needed to feel human in an animalistic environment; for their encouragement and inspiration.

Finally, I love you, Mama, and Greg, too. May the angels in heaven sing at your feet every second of the day. Lord knows life on earth was hell for both of you.

Bill's Acknowledgments

Some of the organizations and individuals whose support and assistance have contributed to the writing of this book include:

The N.A.A.C.P., The Harlem Writers Guild, The National Writers Voice Project, The Writers Voice at the Westside YMCA in New York City, The Fortune Society, The New York Public Library System, The Weeksville Preservation Society, The W.E.B. Du Bois Foundation, The Schomburg Center for Research in Black Culture, WNYE TV, WBAI Radio, Amnesty International, The Unity Democrat Club, The Community Service Society of New York, The United Nations Society of Writers.

The family of Arthur and Marilyn Hamilton, the family of Peter and Adlee Fortune, Dr. John Henrik Clarke, Danny Glover, Rosa Guy, Grace Edwards-Yearwood, Walter Dean Myers, Louise Merriwhether, Prof. Vivian Winley, Prof. David Graham Du Bois, Joan Maynard, Charles L. White, Lucille Lewis, Rev. Jacqueline R. Bullock, Lorressa Crockett, Fred Smith, Jr., Sterling Poitier, Ruby Dee, Esther Jackson, Max Rodriques, Melba Duncan, James Hammond, the Doig family, Glenda Pleasants, Jason Shinder, Pharoah Sanders, Omar Glover, Marie Brooks and family, Sonia Sanchez, Mark Patz, Muriel Wiltord, the Moss family, the Parker family, F.A. Motley, Carolyn Berry, Lawrence Aaron, Oliver Henry, Reynald Louis, Prof. Ethelburt Miller, Marjorie Fortune, Roger Fortune, Marcella Fortune, Sammy Fortune, the Henry family, the Ahmed family, Audrey Jacobs, Vera Wells, the Reid family, A. Chimaranga, Dr. & Mrs. D.P. Graham, Brenda Wilkerson, Donis Ford, Wesley Brown, Betty N. Jackson, Bob DesVergney, the McNatt family, Scott Hamilton, Kathleen Warnock, Catherine Palmer, the Tucker family, Lenore Sampaio, Hans Janitschek, the Pitts family, Charles & Gail Lynch, Debra McCoy, David R. Jones, Cynthia Soslind, Bruce Marcus, the Holzer family, the Glaser family, and Dakari Hru.

And In loving memory of:

William H. Banks, Sr.	Langstroth Fortune
Dorothy Fortune Banks	Bill Williams Ford
Peter Fortune, Sr.	John Oliver Killens
Peter Fortune, Jr.	Audrey Lorde
Mrs. Adlee Fortune	Prof. Sylvia Arden Boone
Hon. Thomas R. Fortune	Luther Bullock, Sr.
Eunice Smith	Luther Bullock, Jr.

Foreword

The most compelling aspect of this story for me is the affirmation of the fact that the human soul cannot be imprisoned. Moreover, the life of Arthur Hamilton, which he virtually lost, recovered, then rebuilt, also shows that the human spirit is most vividly and authentically captured by art. In the case of Arthur, this was and is done with the artistry of the written word.

I have dedicated much of my life to struggling against something which, fortunately, Arthur Hamilton is not faced with—that is, of course, what I believe to be the injustice of the death penalty. But whether you agree with this position or not, anyone should be able to see that Arthur Hamilton's life thus far shows what we all stand to lose if human life is wasted, and it also shows the measure of what people can achieve even after they have lost their freedom. It is clear that Arthur drew upon the lessons of our great forefathers and foremothers, the first African Americans. These were the black people who, even though they came to this country as slaves, have survived and overcome untold hardship as well as created and produced so much that is good for everyone.

Furthermore, Arthur Hamilton's work, in terms of positively guiding the lives of young men who are still in prison, through the columns he writes and the

organization he formed and leads (both named Fathers
Behind Bars), is in the tradition of, if not on the same
scale as, what Nelson Mandela did for South African blacks.
Even before he was released from prison, Mandela led his
people by the strong example of his own survival and his
steadfast dedication to the principles of freedom. Arthur
Hamilton is leading incarcerated young men by stressing
the power and importance of what has both saved and
transformed his life—the love of his family and the
discovery of his ultimate fulfillment in being a father
despite his imprisonment.

If it is true, and I believe that it is, that a lack of love
and understanding imprisons us all to one degree or
another, then I also believe that this story will make
everyone who reads it much freer than they were before.

—Danny Glover
San Francisco, California

Preface

ALL THE WORLD'S A STAGE

All the world's a stage,
And all the men and women merely players:
They have their exits and their entrances;
And one man in his time plays many parts,

—William Shakespeare
As You Like it

One night, as I lay awake in my prison cell, trying to organize my thoughts for this book, I thought about the stage my life had been played upon, and the parts I had played. My entrance had been ill-timed and ill-placed into Detroit's recession-gripped ghettos, and into a family torn apart by abuse and alcoholism. Forced to play parts I was not ready for, forced to stumble across a dark and treacherous stage toward some unknown, bleak conclusion. And as I began to contemplate my exit, a jolt of reality coursed through my body.

I thought about the bums, drunkards, murderers, rapists, and all the other nobodies who have died, and are buried in prison/pauper graves where weeds grow tall and dense, obscuring any sign of their previous existence. And then I thought about the kind of final resting place where loved ones come to place flowers on the graves and talk softly about what those below have left behind. A nice place, a quiet place, a place where people are not ashamed to visit.

And from those two visions grew a desire, a reason, a purpose. I was determined not to leave prison a nobody, buried in a forgotten corner of some forgotten graveyard.

I began to take advantage of the many positive programs that the Michigan prison system had to offer—to throw a few switches, to shed some light on my stage. One achievement led to another, and before I knew it, I began to feel like somebody—a man, a father, a husband, a human being.

I was determined to become as strong as the steel and concrete which separated me from the other "nobodies." I knew I was facing a long stretch in prison. So I steeled myself for the worst that prison had to offer a young, black, inner-city youth. I concreted myself, by bunkering down in books, classrooms, and libraries.

An avalanche of positive ideas and aspirations continued to pour into my mind. Becoming a member of the NAACP taught me the importance of helping others. It was my experience as Chairman of the Press and Publicity Committee at the Kinross Prison Branch NAACP, combined with my new attitude and the prospects of publishing my book, that gave me the inspiration to start an organization that would go beyond issues of race and concentrate instead on fathers in prison, and their children.

I became sensitive to the plight of children who were acting on the same darkened stage that I grew up on. So I founded Fathers Behind Bars Inc., a non-profit organization designed to help the children of incarcerated fathers and to try to keep them from repeating a vicious cycle that sometimes ends with the children sharing the same prison with their fathers. The organization also encourages fathers to become better parents and teaches them to value that role, especially after they are released back into society.

When my cellmate, Darryl Brown, and another friend, Jerome Morton X, decided to make FBB a reality, we vowed to do everything we could to make a difference. My wife, Marilyn, who is also treasurer of FBB, has sacrificed much for the organization, and it shows in the progress that FBB has made. We can only get better.

When I look back in life, I often wonder why I felt like such a failure. I blame no one for my difficult life. I just wish I had matured a lot sooner and dealt with my impulsive behavior in a better way. It would have made a hell of a difference in my life—that's for sure. I could have retired from the Navy in 1996, or maybe from pro-football. The opportunities were there and I blew them.

The opportunities are still there. And this time, for the sake of my family, I will try to use those opportunities to move mountains. I tell my fellow prisoners that I will one day be released from prison, and they will one day look up from a prison auditorium crowd, and think—*we knew him when he played upon a dark and dreary stage, and now we see him on a stage bathed in warm, bright light.*

I will come back to speak to prisoners whenever I am released. I will do everything in my power to reduce the recidivism rate. It is my goal, and with God's help, I will make a difference, and so will FBB, Inc. I want to be living proof that a man can be rescued from hell.

I will continue to conquer each and every one of my goals, one at a time. One of my most important dreams is to one day see all of my children walk across a well-lit stage, inside some college auditorium, with their college degrees clutched proudly in their hands

I also dream of grandchildren, fishing, family reunions... and in the end—flowers. Yes, flowers. Every Sunday, along with a few reassuring words whispered affectionately, long after the curtain has come down, and I have made my exit and gone backstage to the place where my brother and mother are waiting.

Introduction

Early in 1993, I sat in the darkness of a movie theater and had an extremely unnerving experience visited upon me by just one line from the motion picture. The film was *What's Love Got To Do With It: The Ike and Tina Turner Story*. The devastating line was delivered by Ike Turner (played by Lawrence Fishburn) as he viciously berated Tina Turner (played by Angela Bassett) for not wanting to perform her regular singing act because of illness. The line was "...Bitch, you got more excuses than a niggah goin' to jail!"

The line was in keeping with the fascinatingly sinister and unfeeling portrayal of Ike Turner that Fishburn had masterfully conveyed throughout the film. Of course, no one approved of Ike's verbal or physical abuse of Tina. But when he used lines like the one quoted above, his choice of words/weapons was often admired by the audience. (Beautiful black divas in the clutches of villains are to be sympathized with and cheered for, but the same cannot be said for "niggahs goin' to jail.") This probably explained the curious mixture of breathless gasps and muffled giggles that swept across the rows of viewers a moment after the line was uttered.

Ike's words reverberated with me, not because I believed that it accurately described Tina's attitude about her work, but because in the back of my mind, I knew that I was about to become involved with a new book project. One which I thought at the time might very well be nothing more than a compendium of excuses about how yet another poor, broken, and enraged black man had been wrongfully accused, unjustly sentenced, and was now languishing hopelessly in prison. Admittedly, that kind of thing does in fact happen every day, but I did not think that books should be written about it every day, nor was I convinced that, once written, another "prison book" would be received by readers with very much enthusiasm.

This was my state of mind before I met Arthur Hamilton.

Before meeting him, I had little to go on except a very strong letter from the publisher of this book, who wrote, essentially, that he felt he had a great story about a young man in prison who was doing some remarkable things with his life that involved writing. The publisher, Dr. Wayman Spence, was writing to me because he had seen an article about the Harlem Writers Guild in a national publication which mentioned me as the organization's director. The Harlem Writers Guild is a 43-year-old community of writers of African descent who are committed to promoting and preserving the experience of black people in the written word. Some of our alumni include Maya Angelou, John Oliver Killens, Terrie McMillan, and Ossie Davis.

Dr. Spence, whom I found to be as strong and compelling personally as his letter had been to me, suggested that we fly out to meet Arthur in the prison in Michigan. However, a ten-hour flight on three different planes to a cold and desolate place near the Canadian border was not at all appealing. But then I remembered the mission statement of The Harlem Writers Guild... "To promote and preserve the experience of black people in the written word..." I felt that if Dr. Spence, a rangy, Texas physician and businessman who had started his medical career as a prison doctor, had the will to take himself and me out there, then I had the obligation to at least go along. I felt an obligation, but at that point, not much interest in the project.

But it was not until I actually met Arthur Hamilton and his family that I knew that Dr. Spence was even more of a shrewd judge of a great story than he was a salesman. Unlike the angry, embittered, and somewhat confused man that I expected to find, I found an amiable, robust, and secure human being. I found a man who was at peace with himself and the world, even though he faces a sentence which may keep him in prison well into the next century. I found the kind of man that Ike Turner would probably never recognize or appreciate on the most sensitive and sober day of his life. I found a man who made no excuses. I found a man who, with the help of his remarkable wife has built a family life that would be the envy of many. I found a man who, although he is in prison, is consumed with a tremendous passion for his work—and by work I do not mean pressing license plates.

Arthur Hamilton's work is his family, his leadership of other inmates, and his writing.

Father Behind Bars is not a book which deals principally with the horrors of prison life. As a man who is still in prison, there is still much that he cannot say, even though he has not been censored.

This is a story about how one man, and yes, how many men have found their way to prison. Here you will read how changes in society impacted on a single life and probably on many others.

But most of all, you will see how the loss of this man's family contributed to his incarceration more than poverty or so-called criminal influences. And you will see how the restoration of his family saved his life and put him on a mission to help other inmates find their manhood and personhood through the experiences of parenthood and family leadership. Ironically, in terms of the life of Arthur Hamilton and his family, *What's Love Got To Do With It?* is a very important question. The answer is absolutely everything.

Needless to say this is the story of a person of African descent crying out to be preserved in the written word— this is a story that I could not resist.

William H. Banks, Jr.

Chapter 1

NIGHTMARES AND MEMORIES

When my cell door slammed behind me on May 28, 1986, the sound it made was as deathly as the sound of the trapdoor on a gallows. Moreover, I felt just like I was falling with a hangman's noose around my neck. That was the day when the final appeal for the reduction of my sentence was denied. For me, the sentences of twenty-five to fifty years and twelve to fifteen for armed robbery and manslaughter added up to one long *death* sentence. I was nearing the end of my rope and I wanted to take my life.

I'm not special. But I am a man, a male human being, no more and no less. I have learned to withstand imprisonment, to salvage my dignity and my sanity as others have, but the cost was great. The cost has been a tormented soul. A soul tormented by nightmares even more terrible than some of the worst days that I have lived wide-awake on this earth.

In my depression, I descended into a personal hell from which I have not yet entirely returned. It was like falling uncontrollably with a noose around my neck. At any moment, I felt, it would all be over for me. I would find myself at the end of a rope, a bed sheet, my belt, or anything that would support my miserable, worthless weight.

There would be no elaborate plan, no note left to speak for me to a perhaps grieving (but more likely yawning) world. Just a matter of putting something around my neck and tying it to the base of the lamp that was set like an unblinking eye in the ceiling of my cell. Before I would even know what I'd done, I'd be swinging inches above the floor—back and forth, round and round, peering through bulging eyes. Though my eyes would be inflated with desperate, boiling blood, my head would grow colder, as more and more blood vessels were strangled in the same manner as my windpipe.

Withered

I've been in this world,
for a short time.
Countless tears,
wasted,
among the chaos
and riff-raff.

My life is over,
before it has begun.
Yet, why is it,
that I haven't given
up the fight,
to do what is right?

I have travelled the hardest road
of all, but no one
seems to care,
that my life
is but a crawl.

I am a beetle,
scurrying among
the giants.
An ant;
no longer belonging
to a colony.
A bird,
without a nest.

My seeds have
been wasted,
before they have tasted,
the love,
of their manufacturer.
Forgive me Lord,
I am a weary
insect.
I have had a
taste of hell; its
evil inhabitants,
the putrid smell.

Forgive me Lord,
for I am not meant
to be
in this world of
confusion,
where the dreams
of others, are only my illusions.

Forgive me Lord,
I leave no bitterness,
no worldly possessions,
just a fleeing
tenderness; replaced
by bitterness.

The hopes and dreams,
which came so fast,
can only be a rendition,
of my sordid past.

Behold! I have given
myself to prayer
and hope.
Apparently it is
not to be.
So I pray "Dear Giant,
step on me."

What follows my request,
is a deadly sin,
but in this lifetime,
I cannot win.
God, save us all,
and farewell
to hell.

In my nightmare, I am hanging, spinning around
slowly, looking at my ten by eight foot cell—first the bars
on the door, then my bunk and the toilet, then the bars
on the window, then the bare wall, then the bars on the
door again. All these things would go in and out of focus
as my body twisted round and round.

Each time the end differs. Sometimes I would just swing
there at the end of the rope until darkness closed in on
me. But most often, the last thing I would see was the
faces of the other inmates at my cell door. Somehow, the
face of every guy in the joint was there watching me.
Prisoners, guards, cooks—no bodies, just faces, faces
floating in the darkness behind the bars.

When I first started dreaming this nightmare of suicide,
the faces would scream. They would scream for someone
to open my cell and cut me down. They'd scream for me
to hold onto my life and not give up. But then, night
after night, the floating faces' protests were fewer and
fewer, and the expressions on their faces became blanker
and blanker until they became glazed, vague sketches of
human features.

Finally, the voices were silent, the faces gone, the bars
gone—replaced by an enormous array of shelves, lined
with empty, silent skulls. The momentum of my swinging
body dissipated, I faced a wall of skulls, an immense wall

of gray skulls that dwarfed even the memory of the cell door from which it had grown.

I was born Arthur Lee Hamilton, Jr., October 19, 1957, in Detroit, Michigan. I was born the son of an alcoholic father who abused my mother until she fled from him with her four children during a cold winter day in the year 1965. Though never exactly saying so, we all privately prayed that Mama was leaving the beatings behind. It was this meager hope and not our meager clothing that shielded us the most from the cold.

The snow was deep in Detroit that day, and we trudged through it until we arrived at my aunt Sarah's home. Aunt Sarah owned a two-story house from which my other Aunt, whose name was Rebecca, had just moved. The timing seemed perfect for my mother and her shivering brood.

The distance from my father's house to the new place on Tyler Street was only about a mile, but in the deep and driving snow, it took us three hours. We had each grabbed as much of the collective burden as we could individually carry. That included, of course, the collective pain my father had caused us. I carried a paper bag full of clothes, half dragging it through the snow. About a third of the way through the trip, the bag ripped open and the clothes spilled out onto the ground. The red of my brother's pajamas, the blue of our blue jeans and the yellow of a summer shirt lying on the ground in front of me were the only colors that I remember seeing that day. I remember seeing the colors and the clothes quickly disappear as the driving snow buried them.

As my mother helped me gather the scattered clothes and stuff some of them into a bundle she had, she wiped away my tears, kissed me, and consoled all of us with the reassurance that we were headed for a better place. We pushed on once again.

Carrying the clothes in my arms turned out to be a blessing. Holding it in front of my face and in front of my chest helped to keep me warm. My brother and sisters watched me and did as I did. We all clung to our bundles for warmth and protection, just as later, we would cling to our mother in what we all dearly hoped really was that "better place" she had spoke of.

Several times after that, I fell in the snow. But most of the time I would get up before my mother would see me lying behind her. The obvious pain in her face whenever she did turn around made me know that this was it—I had to grow up right then and there in the midst of that storm. Impossible as it might have seemed, I had to become a man—albeit an eight-year-old man—for the sake of my family.

I looked over at my sister Gale. She, like the rest of us, seemed to be just a tattered little stick figure struggling against the wind and snow. Though only a couple of feet away from her, I could just barely see her face and there wasn't much to see. Unlike my mother's face, which showed mostly anguish, Gale's face showed mostly nothing, not even hurt or pain, just a blank stare looking straight forward into the storm. She barely even blinked— even when snow got into her eyes. I always felt that she knew something, something that older kids know, but don't tell stupid little kids who would either not understand or, even worse, would start crying if they were told.

Then I looked at my little brother Greg. We all knew that he carried the heaviest load: a bad pair of lungs nestled next to what must have been one of the sweetest and strongest little hearts in the world. Just a month earlier, he had nearly died of pneumonia. He had had it and meningitis twice, and my mother worried about him most. Little Greg held on to my frayed coat and carried a small bundle. We continued moving forward. At one point I remember that he started coughing very hard and we took temporary shelter in the doorway of a church. "You see?... The Lord will always protect us if we're honest and we keep the faith," my mother said as we paused in the doorway while she wiped the snow off of Greg's back. Gale's expression told me that she was not converted by my mother's brief sermon. Instead, Gale turned from our small, huddled group, peered back out into the storm, sighed, and tightened her overcoat (which she had outgrown) around herself.

Little Greg's burden (his poor health) may have been the heaviest burden but one of Mama's bundles was without a doubt the most precious. Mama carried my baby sister Tracy. Mercifully, Tracy had slept every step of the way snugly wrapped inside of who knows how many assorted blankets.

Once back out in the storm Greg began to speak for all of us when he asked: "Mama where are we? ... When will we get there?"

"We're almost there and we'll get there soon." She said to us. But from the way she craned her long graceful neck to squint through the snow at street signs, we could not be sure. Of course, running with our mother from our father's abuse in a blinding snow storm, we couldn't be sure of anything. We knew what we were running from but not what we were running to.

Many times, many years since then, I have wished, while alone in my cell at Marquette Maximum Security Prison, that we had never made it through that storm.

Yes, I've actually wished that we had just perished as a family right then and there in that storm rather than accept and play the hand that life was about to place on the table in front of us. Strange to believe perhaps, but such are the depraved musings of a tormented soul.

After what seemed like the longest extended period of time in the whole journey, my mother's voice rang excitedly in our near-frozen ears: "There's the house!— There's your Aunt Sarah's house!"

Sure enough, less than fifty feet away from where we stood at that moment was a house... the same house that mama had described to us in glowing and hopeful terms. We cheered and started to run the rest of the way. But our numb feet and legs could not keep pace with our new enthusiasm. Moreover, the still mounting snow seemed to suck our legs and feet to the ground. The faster we tried to move, the quicker we sank into the snow. It was as though we were in slow motion. Our frustration gave way to laughter, and we laughed and giggled at each other's playful plight. If anyone in Detroit needed and deserved a good laugh, it was us.

We rounded the corner of the pathway that led to the

front door. Once again my mother's voice rang out triumphantly above the sound of the howling wind as she read the address on the door—2679 Tyler. "Hallelujah! Praise God, Praise his Holy name," my mother said as she led her band of weary Christian soldiers up to Aunt Sarah's door. The wind blew harder and snow started to come down heavier, but it didn't matter anymore... We were THERE.

We assembled at the front door. My mother quieted us down before she knocked on the door. She banged that door for ten minutes before she started crying, knuckles red and swollen. Then she pounded on every window in the house. No one was home.

Chapter 2

MAMA DIDN'T LIE

We waited there for what seemed like hours, just freezing in that storm. My mother kept telling us that it was just some mistake and that our aunt would soon be home to let us in. My aunt did come home, of course, but it wasn't soon.

That was the problem. As good sounding and as near perfect as whatever Mama might have said to us was, there always seemed to be a hitch. It took the three of us many sad years to learn this. If you include my mother's life before we were born, you see that she lived many sad years. But she never learned anything from this hardship, and since she never lied to us, we always believed Mama no matter what.

If the address was right then nobody was home. If God had brought us through the storm then it was just barely. If the somebody was home, then, well the problem would be something like the rats were home too. And if mama said: "It's time to eat," then she spoke to the rats that were in that house as well as to her children. Some of the rats we found at Aunt Rebecca's house were as big as cats and therefore not much smaller than us kids.

Mama would battle them all the time—morning, noon, and night. It would never stop. The sound of her swatting at them with anything she could find permeated and punctuated everything: getting dressed (rats would scatter each time we opened a closet), sleeping (sometimes their squealing sounded like talking or even laughter), and eating. This is when the battle between us and the rats was the most vicious. It was war.

The rats would smell the food and try to take it from us, waiting until my mother had left the room for something or perhaps just turned her back from the table to use the sink or go to the refrigerator. Then they'd go into action. They would climb up the leg of our kitchen table and sit right there at the edge of it and stare at us and the food. The sight of them with their miserable little, cold shiny eyes and twitching, whiskered little snouts would drive us away from the table in fright. Then they would attack our food.

I remember tripping over rats who were running to the table as I was running from it. Once up on the table leg, some of the rats were content with devouring morsels of our chicken, hamburger, peas, corn or beans off the plates. Others, usually the bigger ones, would try to haul the food away. By that I mean, they would grab hold of say... half a chicken! and drag it or push it off the table, where a growing swarm of the rodents waiting to either feast on the spot or to drag the food off to a hidden lair.

They moved fast. They had to because they knew from experience they didn't have much time. They knew that although our screams signaled our retreat, it also soon thereafter heralded my mother's attack. Mama would go at them with any club-like contrivance that she could fashion. Rolled-up newspapers and magazines were her favorite though. And she would weal her paper clubs like the hammer of Thor. And the rats would drop the food and run for cover.

The rats had an advantage in that for the most part they could run faster than Mama. But when she did get one, there was cause for excitement and momentary relief. Usually the first blow was not a direct hit. It would only stun the rat. It would slow down just enough for Mama to hit it again and again until finally it would lay there motionless and presumably lifeless. I say presumably because I remember once Mama thought that she had knocked one out or killed one. But she was wrong.

After hitting one rat several times, Mama sighed with relief as if killing one of them would somehow frighten the rest off forever. Hoarsely, she whispered something like "Lord have mercy!" as she poked at the rodent's body to confirm its death. Suddenly, a row of tiny snarling teeth appeared at the base of the rat's hairy snout. The two little, cold shiny eyes blinked then squinted. Before my mother could lift her paper club to strike another blow, the rat twisted itself around and bit Mama viciously on her arm, then sprinted to safety behind the refrigerator.

Mama stared in disbelief at the blood on her arm. "Get me some Mercurochrome," she said calmly.

We scampered to do her bidding. When we got to the medicine cabinet my two sisters, my brother, and I looked into it and then sadly at each other. There was no mercurochrome, no iodine, no ointment of any kind except a small bottle of rubbing alcohol.

We brought the bottle to her and we watched as she poured the alcohol over her bleeding arm. The pain created by the alcohol must have been more terrible than the ordeal with the rat. For the first time that day, and moreover, for the first time since we had come through the storm together to that rat infested, God-forsaken, "better place," my mother cried. We brought her a towel but she pushed it away reminding us that we only owned *two* towels in the whole world. "Just bring some toilet paper," she instructed. "And don't bring too much. We don't have much of that or of anything else that's useful... 'cept maybe the Lord. The Lord is all we got."

My mother bit her lip and poured some more alcohol. She pressed the toilet paper to the wounds and breathed deeply. She hugged us tightly with both her wounded arm and her exhausted arm, too. We kissed her and she smiled a bit. We wanted to smile back, but I don't think we did. As great as my mother's battle and victory was, the truth was that it was only one rat—one rat with maybe a million more to go. But my mother smiled with satisfaction.

Mama breathed deeply again. This time she squinted, then stared off as if she was remembering something. Either she could see what we were thinking and feeling through our eyes, or maybe after some moments she had finally remembered the fullness of our poverty. "Bad as this is it's not as bad as it was," she told us, and she was right.

The smell of the alcohol had reminded all of us of the way things had been before.

Chapter 3

CRIME AND REVOLUTION

I have been incarcerated for the past eleven years. During that time, I have seen thousands of young men come into prison, leave, and unfortunately in many cases, return. For a long time, I thought that what I had in common with them and what all the incarcerated people have in common was poverty. "If they won't let a black man work and make it, then he's got to get out there in the mean streets and steal and take it." If someone had set that saying to music, it could have been both the anthem and philosophy of a whole nation of black men like me. But all that was far too simple.

Criminals and unconvicted wrongdoers are vastly outnumbered in this country, and probably in the world, by poor people who will commit few if any crimes in their lives. Moreover, many, perhaps most, wrongdoers are never caught, tried, or convicted. For them, crime does seem to pay, as comparatively few of them are poor. And non-poor people seldom find themselves as far as I am on the wrong side of the criminal justice system. But for the guys like me, who were born poor, who do wrong, and are caught and convicted, what set *us* on the path to prison? Not just poverty.

Whenever human rights are abused by individuals within a society, revolutionaries are often spawned. Unfortunately, whenever those same rights are abused within a family, criminals are very often created. That's where I come from.

My home was not destroyed by society. Although society did and does pitifully little to help folks like we were. Instead my family was destroyed by a single individual, my father.

There is a line of thinking which dictates that the dysfunction found in some black families is a reflection of, and possibly a direct result of, white oppression. Take all the racial discrimination in the world today, multiply this by all the discrimination against the black man since the dawn of slavery, and put this entire burden squarely on the shoulders of my father—do all of this, and you still won't have justification for the beatings he gave Mama, or the way he ignored his children.

Using violence and the threat of violence to control people is not uncommon and not incomprehensible. But my father used violence not just as a way of control but also as a way of *communicating*. Violence was his vocabulary, his syntax, his grammar, and his intonation. It was as pervasive as the rats in the house on Tyler Street and as brutal as the snow storm we endured getting there.

We were not a "broken home," like once-liberal social workers designated them. (You remember the paradigm of the "broken home" don't you? That's where the father leaves the home so that the unfathered unit he deserts can get welfare. Meanwhile, this erstwhile dude can plant his soulful seed throughout the firmament of the ghetto, creating more "broken homes.")

Believe me, a man who was no more harmful or helpful than a sperm-laden ghetto version of Johnny Appleseed would have not been welcome by my mother with either open arms or legs. My mother was fiercely and in most respects a "family values" person. (Now before right wing conservatives start cheering too loudly, let me say something. It's clear to me now that creating civilized, non-criminal behavior in children involves the successful transmission of human values—like not brutalizing people either physically, mentally, or emotionally—from one generation to the next within the family setting. Please note that I said "human values" not "family values" even though the transmission is done in the family.)

But if a such Johnny Applesperm had come along, and he had been otherwise decent and above all, he had been good to her kids, she might have given him a chance. The trouble is she never got far enough away from my father and his brutality until it was too late in our lives.

Our home was not "broken"—it was "battered." I came from a family that was literally pummeled out of existence.

It would have been better if my father *had* left us. My mother could have raised us just fine. Poor as we were, she could have done a very fine job raising us by herself— even though we were a handful. But the worst of her many mistakes was staying with my father as long as she did. This was the mistake that undermined much of the many good things that she did do for us.

In many senses I'm probably the last person you should ask where my road to prison began. But I have a theory— Was the beginning when my brother Greg and I put phony money in the collection plate at church so that we would have money to buy candy?—Was it when I pulled my first armed robbery?—Was it when I killed the man who sold little children drugs?—No, by those times, and at those stages of crime, I had already fallen by the proverbial wayside and was already headed toward this hell. The beginning for me was when my father finally mentally pounded out of me any sense of self-worth or sense of caring for other people.

My first criminal act was imitating my father—not his crimes but his violence.

Chapter 4

SCENE OF THE CRIMES:
DETROIT

The drama of my life of crime was played out in the theater of the city of Detroit. Detroit's decline was intertwined with the fortunes of hundreds of thousands of people who were mostly black and far from affluent in the first place. Before I ever thought of pulling a gun, circumstances and forces were coming into play in Detroit that made my criminal career and that of many other black men almost inevitable.

When I was born in 1957, Detroit was one of the great cities of the country. Filled with virtually all races of people it was a proud, muscular, hard-working, blue-collar giant of a city. Like all cities there was, of course, racism, and we (poor black people) felt it acutely. We were consigned to the decrepit, rundown section of the city appropriately, if not affectionately, known as Black Bottom. And that consignment was to be our lot.

Other races and ethnic groups lived in different neighborhoods of Detroit, but that kind of segregation was more subtle than, for example, in the South. The divisions were based on ethnocentric patterns and family traditions that went back generations. People lived wherever "their people" (meaning both blood relations and people of the same ethnic group) lived.

Detroit's white politicians controlled all of this by virtue of their control of city government. They determined where housing of various quality and types were built, and that virtually kept the demographic patterns of the neighborhoods ethnic groups intact and more or less divided.

My studies of Detroit politics have revealed that in that city, just as around the country, keeping neighborhoods white was a silent but important political issue. Even the threat of the presence of blacks in a white neighborhood could cause property values to plunge, along with the political fortunes of local politicians who needed the votes of the scared, but not necessarily racist, white home owners.

This tight, if not blatant control of the city's demographic landscape by white politicians was masked by completely open and integrated public accommodations. We (poor black folk like my family) could go anywhere we wanted to go in Detroit without having to ride on the back of any bus or train. The problem instead was we often didn't have the fare.

Different ethnic groups lived more or less peacefully in adjoining but still clearly separated neighborhoods in Detroit. This was defacto segregation, of course, but it was not the blatant kind of racism that was rampant in the South at that time. That kind of racism and segregation was supported by laws shaped by a white Southern attitude that was still fighting the Civil War.

In 1954, three years before I was born, the South was turned upside down by the Supreme Court's Brown vs. Board of Education decision which led to the integration of public schools in Little Rock, Arkansas, a place not two-hundred miles from where the current president of the United States, Bill Clinton, was then living as a boy.

My mother told me years later of watching the federal troops on TV that year. She and the world watched troops, that had been activated, not by Arkansas' governor, Orville

Forbus, but by the nation's president, Dwight D. Eisenhower, sweep into that sleepy little town (where some black folks that we knew had come up to Detroit from) and wake up the monster of white Southern racism. The federal troops did put black children in the Little Rock schools, but the whole affair put no brotherly love in the hearts of racist, white Southerners, and likewise no knowledge of or respect for the American Constitution in their heads.

Three years later, the year I was born, Emmet Till, a black kid from Chicago, was brutally murdered, while on vacation in Mississippi, for allegedly whistling at a white girl down there. For years, my mother kept the pictures that appeared in *Jet* magazine (Bless the soul of Mr. John H. Johnson, *Jet's* publisher) of Emmet Till's bloated and decayed body that was pulled out of the Mississippi River. As kids, these pictures were part of our earliest education about the existence, meaning, and deadliness of racism.

The rest of America, including our town of Detroit, shook it's head at what it saw in the South in those days. But maybe instead of shaking their collective heads, what people in Detroit and the rest of the country should have done was to look around at their own surroundings.

Though segregation by law was no longer legal anywhere, segregation in fact existed just about everywhere. And as I pointed out, Detroit was no exception.

As the 1950's turned into the '60s, I grew up, and the movement for racial equality moved out of the South. The patterns of discrimination in places like Detroit, even though not blatantly racist, were being recognized and tensions were growing between blacks and whites. Sadly, blacks were beginning to recognize these patterns of discrimination and whites were beginning to defend them.

It was as though black people everywhere were beginning to catch up to the wisdom of Malcolm X. During the late '50s and early '60s, when the spotlight of public attention was almost exclusively on the racism in the Deep South, Malcolm X observed: "When it comes to racism in America there is only one 'South' and that is everything south of Canada."

VERNON REGIONAL
JUNIOR COLLEGE LIBRARY

Other things began to negatively affect Detroit as well at this time.

The great blue-collar giant that was Detroit, which stood on the banks of Lake Superior, was beginning to experience heart palpitations. This was because within the chest of that giant was a heart which, until that time, had been the greatest automotive production entity the world had ever known.

Smaller, more efficient cars, mostly made by the Japanese, were destroying the American dream of the American autoworker. Worse than the loss of a dream, this economic Pearl Harbor was a living nightmare for poor blacks.

The auto industry was the greatest hope and the most frequent savior of poor blacks like we were. The work and the money that came from helping to make cars, no matter how menial an auto plant job might have been, was one of the few things that was both real and obtainable. We could see that we were a part of the phenomena of the American automobile. Blacks *owned* cars if not homes, decent or otherwise. Moreover, it seemed that everybody, or at least anybody who was able-bodied and hard-working, could get some kind of job in either a plant or a related business.

It also seemed that before the advent of the preeminence of Japanese cars, everyone from our local, black-culture royalty of show-business people, such as the Temptations, to the everyday man or woman in the street, had worked or could have worked in the car industry. All of that was changing.

By the mid '60s, jobs and white people were leaving Detroit in droves. Jobs were going to Japan and whites were moving to Michigan suburbs. Interestingly enough, one of the few growth industries in rural areas during that time was prison construction. Virtually overnight, white, ethnic, working-class neighborhoods in Detroit became impoverished black ghettos.

The loss of population and tax revenue was devastating for Detroit. Services shrunk, and of course for us they all but disappeared. In schools, class size grew as attendance plummeted. Soon school closings were epidemic. Streets became dirty and dangerous as sanitation workers and cops struck, not for higher wages, but to keep their jobs. The police force became embittered, embattled, and overburdened. Police brutality increased and black resistance smoldered. The aging, white city fathers grew gray and retired with their fleeing constituents to the suburbs.

By 1967, the tenth year of my life, much of Detroit was in flames.

When the embers finally cooled and the smoke blew away, thousands of units of housing had disappeared. What had appeared, even before the riot of '67, was drugs. The height of the Vietnam War was approaching. The loss of young black men in the war was matched only by the loss of young black males due to drugs.

The only good memories I have from that period was the music. The music of The Supremes, The Temptations, The Miracles, The Four Tops, Stevie Wonder, and others made the Music of Motown. The Motown Sound was dubbed by it's creator, the gifted impresario Mr. Barry, "The Sound of Young America." And so it was.

I loved the music, but it meant even more to others. It captured the best hopes and the honest restlessness of the generation just before mine. This is the youngest generation that remembers President Kennedy and Martin Luther King; the generation of Bill Clinton—the baby boomers. I was just a kid in the era of the Motown Sound, but the baby boomers came of age with it.

But then in the early '70s, even the music died in Detroit. That's when Mr. Gordy, and all the wonderful music that his company had created for almost twenty years, left Detroit for the emerging Sunbelt. The musical empire that had been born in perhaps the greatest working-class city in America would now make it's home in Hollywood, California, with the laid back and pampered Beautiful People.

The blow to the psyche of kids growing like me in Detroit then was and is unforgettable. The blow to our spirit was as severe as the loss of the auto industry to the economy of the city. The Motown public relations people tried to put a good face on Mr. Gordy's motives when they claimed that Motown was entering a new phase, that it wanted to enter the movie industry—Yeah, right—Motown moved out there over twenty years ago and Diana Ross, Motown's only real movie star, only made two movies, and she has since left Motown.

There is a Motown music company today, but as for my generation of black kids from Detroit, that Motown might as well be in Japan with the export car industry, and they might as well be singing or rapping or whatever it is they do today in Japanese. Motown left Detroit for greener (as in money) pastures and whiter (as in money) people.

Earlier I said that poverty alone would not send people into a life of crime. But the poverty of spirit and mind, as well as that of the pocketbook (such as we encountered in the midst of the decline of Detroit) can indeed set a person on a path to self-destruction.

Chapter 5

A BOY'S LIFE IN OLD DETROIT

Even though we were poor, I can't say that we had exactly nothing. And more importantly, even though we were black, I certainly cannot say we lived lives that were consumed with only the ravages of racism. We were deeply loved, and up to and even sometimes beyond the limits of our mother's meager resources, we were well taken care of and protected.

When I was little, I seldom had a chance to go anywhere because Mama was always at work and my grandma and aunt were strict as hell. Because of hard times, we seldom had money to do anything, so when I asked my mother if I could go to movies in downtown Detroit with the kids next door, she said "No."

I begged Mama to let me go. It was a big deal for a ghetto kid to get to go to the downtown movie theatres. I cried and pleaded. I'll never forget the look on her face, when she broke down and told me she didn't have enough money. Except for her lunch and bus fare, she was broke.

"Besides, you don't have any clothes for going downtown. I'm not going to let you go looking like a bum."

I darted up to my bedroom and dug out some old clothes that my half-brother Bruce had left when he had visited us the summer before. There was even a pair of shoes. The Sharpskinned pants practically swallowed my small frame—I used a gigantic safety pin to hold them up. I stuffed the size eleven shoes with toilet paper, put them on my size eight feet, and went down to show Mama.

Mama burst out laughing.

Seeing how bad I wanted to go, she gave me her lunch money. I often wonder, now, how many times she did without herself in order to please us kids.

A car horn sounded. I ran outside, leaving Mama mumbling something about how crazy I was dressed. I leapt off the porch, bypassing the steps, and losing a shoe in the process. I could hear the neighbors laughing in the car as I tried to stuff the toilet paper back into the shoe. All of a sudden it hit me that I must have looked like Bozo the clown or something in that ridiculous outfit.

Mama was standing at the door, no longer laughing. The look on her face was a painful mixture of embarrassment and helplessness. I realized then how much I hated being poor.

Shoes for the Children

See the po' child
no shoes on his feet.
Hair so nappy
as he plays in the street.

Po' Po' child
ain't got no one.
Don't know what it means
to have real fun.

You come out yo' house
see him playing in the street.
Just shake yo' head,
keep walking to the beat.

Well, you'll pay
for ignoring that boy someday.
What goes around, comes back,
in some worse way.

He goes to school empty,
good intentions to learn.
But the drug dealer yells,
"IT'S YOUR TURN!!!"

In my pre-teen youth, Detroit was a great town for
kids. Before the crime rate started to soar it was like an
entire country (it was in fact our whole world) and we
treated it like our own uncharted land and we (mostly
my brother Greg and I) became explorers. Our explorer
ships were one or two bikes (we rode two on a bike if one
was broken), and we'd ride all over town. There were still
safe neighborhoods and safe passages and times to go
through rougher neighborhoods back then.

Trouble, of course, existed then, just as it did years
later when things really started to get bad, but at least in
those days you knew where the trouble was and how to
avoid it. Mama always worried about her little boys, but
Mama always worked long hours, so there was only so
much that she could do to restrict our wandering when
she was away from home.

We'd ride to see the parts of the city we'd only heard
of or maybe the parts that we wanted to see again. Like
the great sports stadiums where the Tigers played baseball
and the Lions played football were a favorite of ours. If
there was a game going on, we'd stop and watch the
great masses of people going in or coming out. We'd
often speculate about what would happen if there was
some kind of stampede or something. We thought it
would be something like the stampedes on the old TV
Westerns except the urban kind would have people instead
of cattle. We never saw a stampede of course, but it was
still fun to watch and imagine.

We also enjoyed just lingering outside the stadiums to
rest and enjoy a soda or some candy. Real excitement
came during these respites if we were outside when a big
play was made in the game. The roar that came out of

the stadiums can almost not be described. It sounded like a million voices to us. In the spring and summer when we heard the roar, we'd hope that maybe a guy had hit a home run, and that it would come sailing over the wall, and we'd get it, and it would be the biggest hit of the guy's career, and we'd get the ball, and we'd take it to him, and he'd be real happy, and he'd take pictures with us, and we'd be on television, and everybody else would see us, and we'd get famous, and we'd get lots of money, and we'd be real happy—but, of course, that ball never came over that wall.

As for actually going to see games, we didn't do that too often; money, of course, was the reason. I remember one day, while we were resting on our bikes waiting for that home run that never came, I promised Greg that I'd get him inside a game, later on, when Mama thought that I was old enough to have a paper route.

Whenever both our bikes were broken and/or Mama was not at work, we would all invariably be close to home.

There was fun and adventure there too sometimes.

Sometimes it was the dangerous kind.

Once, when I was fourteen, after we had moved from Tyler Street, I came under the spell of an older guy who had been a real life, black, flesh and blood soldier. Not the white, plastic G.I. Joe kind that Greg and I had been used to playing with for most of our youth.

This man was a veteran of the early stages of the Vietnam War. He was a Marine who had served with distinction in several parts of Southeast Asia. This guy, I'll call him Ken, was highly regarded in our neighborhood. All veterans were similarly well thought of in most places at that time. This was well before the troop build-up in Southeast Asia which ultimately lead to the unpopularity that would later characterize the Vietnam conflict.

Ken was a colorful guy who liked to dress in full military regalia. His customary attire included, of course, his Lincoln-green beret (which he wore constantly and always at a roguish tilt), sharply pressed and pristine fatigues, and spit shined, dress combat boots that gleamed like glistening black coals. Ken was tall and muscular in a lanky sort of way. And in uniform, he reminded us of Woody Strode. That is, if Woody had ever been allowed to portray a commanding officer in a movie, which he wasn't.

Ken would pace back and forth under a tree in his backyard and describe to us kids in the most forceful manner and to the most minute detail, the nature of all his combat exploits. He would carry a drumstick (the kind you use to beat drums, not the chicken kind you eat) tightly in one hand or tucked under his arm. This was his substitute for a commanding officer's baton. We kids didn't know this, but to us, it might as well have been a magic wand and Ken, a magician.

Part of Ken's magic was that we would believe anything he said and we'd do just about anything he asked us to do. Ken rarely asked us to do more than listen to his stories and promise to enlist in the Marine Corps within seconds after our seventeenth birthdays.

But on this one day back then, Ken was intent upon teaching us how he had helped wipe countless "Slope Head Cong" and how he was making use of his military proficiency on the Detroit home front.

"I'm gonna really show you cats about some serious combat today," Ken said as he put a shovel into my hands as well as the hands of Greg and two of our friends. There was a curious and intense gleam in his eyes that day, as bright as the shine on his boots, and as mysterious as the power he held over our young minds.

"I'm also gonna show you how to fuck up some mother fuckers today, too!" He said while striding briskly over to his garage.

"What are these shovels for?" I asked.

"Oh..." Ken said matter-of-factly without breaking his military stride. "First we gotta dig a big foxhole."

And so we dug. Right there in Ken's backyard we dug a hole so deep the four of us kids could stand in it. We packed the dirt in a parameter around the hole and just stood there looking at Ken who was sweating and smiling. He still had that gleam in his eyes.

"Okay, you cats hop in there and wait!" He said pointing to the foxhole.

"Get in there and stay ready." He said as he got into his car. "I'll be right back... I got to make a run real quick."

Just as Ken was about to pull out of the backyard his mother, who had been watching us through a window since we entered the backyard, raised the window and shouted:

"Kenny... have you taken your meditation like you're supposed to?"

Ken shifted gears and stepped on the clutch while he looked up to his mother and said: "No Ma... I ain't took no meditation cause the damn VA doctor didn't prescribe no meditation for me to take, and I ain't gonna take no more of that damn medication he did prescribe 'cause that stuff just messes up my mind." With that Ken popped the clutch and sped through the driveway and out to the street where he shifted again. He burned rubber, smoking for about a half a block.

Ken's mother shook her head as she closed the window saying something like: "Lord have mercy."

Inside the foxhole we waited, at first, somewhat nervously. We wondered what in the world could be going on. As times passed our nervousness was abated by other things. For one thing, we argued among ourselves about whether Ken was going to really do something with us there at the foxhole or whether he was going to come back and pick us up and maybe take us on some kind of real exciting maneuver in that real cool car he had. While taking bets on what was going to happen next we praised Ken and admired him for standing up to his mother the way he had. We figured it took a lot of nerve seeing as Ken was living right there in his mother's house. We just couldn't wait to grow up and be just like Ken.

Of all the things we talked about, we never even considered or talked about leaving that foxhole; that just goes to show you how dumb we were.

About forty-five minutes later, we heard Ken's screeching tires in the driveway again.

Ken jumped out of the car and ran into the garage. "Stay low!" Ken commanded from the garage. We hit our knees. We couldn't see now but we heard Ken's footsteps running toward us in the foxhole. Then we heard Ken's mother shouting:

"Kenny what are you going to do with those guns?"

Crouched down together we looked into each other's eyes and started trembling with fear.

I looked up just in time to see my hero handing me a rifle. He gave each one of us a rifle and then we listened in stunned silence as our leader spoke:

"We used to do this shit all the time over in Nam!" Ken said. "First we'd engage some slope head Congs in a little fight then we'd lead their asses into an ambush like this... All we got to do is wait... I went over to the Ferndale side of Eight Mile Road and shot up the house of some mother fucker who been fuckin' wid me... He and his boys are haulin' ass over here now to get me, but won't be expecting this... When they get here follow my lead. Blast they asses with these M1's you're holdin'... Got It?"

We couldn't speak. We just squatted there in fear wondering if we'd ever get out alive. When Ken turned to peek out of the foxhole, I saw what looked like a bullet hole in the back of his beret. I would later learn that it was nothing but an old cigarette burn.

The last thing I remember Ken doing was ripping off that beret, thrusting his middle finger through that hole and saying with his biggest grin of the day:

"Hey come back next week and I'll show you guys how soldiers get pussy."

Ya know what? That's just what we did.

Chapter 6

GREG

Other than my mother, my present wife and my children, my brother Greg was my strongest connection to this life. The bond between us was as strong as the connection to life that his existence provided me with.

Even in conflict this bond was virtually indestructible. Once when we were kids, I wanted to go off and play football with some older boys. There was no place for Greg in this because he was younger and so much weaker than the other guys, and I and because he had made it clear that he wasn't willing to just watch me play with other guys. What Greg wanted was what he almost always had had before, and that was to have me all to himself.

After arguing with him for awhile, I screamed at him to leave me alone and to go home. Greg hauled off and socked me as hard as he could right on the chin. It felt like little more than a tap to me, but Greg had put everything in his frail little body into that punch. The other guys wanted me to hit him back to put him in his place—I had the urge to do it too, but not because he had hurt me or for reasons of ego, but because for a moment, that little punch reminded me of my father, and for that scant moment, my brother's modest facial resemblance to my father increased ten fold. Then in a flash he was little Greg again, and the momentary animosity that I had felt for him evaporated.

Greg stood there trembling with rage for many moments, then he turned and ran away crying. My new friends, the big boys, thought this was funny, even hilarious. This amused them so much that it delayed the game of football while they laughed. One of them asked facetiously if Greg was a boy or a girl because of his crying.

By the time the guys had settled down to play I was already running... running to catch Greg. My legs pumped harder and harder beneath me as my speed picked up but I was hardly aware of it. My mind had become a split screen of desperate images. I saw Greg getting hit by a car, I saw Greg getting beat up by gangs and I saw my mother and sisters in tears. It was so real that the clear light of day could not penetrate what I was conjuring in my mind. I almost ran smack dab into a car myself.

From that point, with Greg nowhere in sight, I ran straight home. When I arrived, Greg was there with Mama. She sat the bowl of tuna fish aside that she was preparing for supper and took us aside. I remember clearly that she held both my hands in her right hand and both Greg's hands in her left hand as she spoke.

First she turned to Greg and said to him: "Gregory, Artie is your brother, he always will be your brother and he loves you, but he's entitled to have some friends of his own... even if these boys weren't good friends." Then she turned to me and said: "You are the man of this house, and most important, you are your brother's keeper." Then she put both of my hands together with both of Greg's and squeezed them as if to seal them together forever.

Then she sent Greg away and then said to me: "Being a man means keeping promises... It's time for you to start keeping some of yours." She said that now was the time for me to get that paper route so I could earn the money to keep the promise I had made to Greg, to take him to the Tigers and Lions games, and to help out around the house.

That's what I started doing. I worked my ass off on that route. Having already ridden all over the city with Greg on our bikes meant that I knew the city so well, I could get a route anywhere and do well, and I did. Some of my routes even spilled over into the white communities. I was a working man. A working man of ten who could fulfill his promises to his little brother and contribute money to the household like a real "Man of the House" should do.

Then one day I came to work and my boss told me that I had lost my job. He gave no reason. He just said that it was over and I was finished. I told my mother and she called him. He said there was some kind of cutback or something. It was such an obvious lie that the guy didn't even really want to talk to my mother. He practically hung up on her. My mother said that she was going to "pray on" the situation to get my job back. I got on my bike.

Over the course of the next several days I went to locations on each route at the time of the scheduled deliveries. The deliveries were made just as I had made them. There was no cutback. The deliveries were being made all right, they were being made by white boys.

Of the five or six kids that I talked to, only three would tell me their names. Those three had the same Polish last name, the same last name as my ex-boss, and they had taken all the routes I had had previously in their communities.

I watched those guys for days after that. I watched them as they went through *my* route, delivering *my* papers to *my* customers and collecting *my* money. It was a simple job but they didn't do it as well as I had. These guys couldn't roll up the papers tightly like I did and they often missed the porches of the customers. They were terrible. They didn't deserve my job. At first I thought I would kick each guy's little white ass and take my job back. Then I thought I'd rob each one on collection day and get *my* money. But then I realized that I had spoken to each guy and they'd snitch and they'd know it was me and I'd get caught. I didn't steal but I sure wanted to.

I told my mother everything (except the part about wanting to beat and rob the white guys) and she said that it was too bad that they didn't have an N.A.A.C.P. for paper boys. She told me that I should keep looking for another job and that she would pray.

I don't know whether it was persistence or prayer, but something worked. Greg and I were racing shopping carts in the parking lot outside of a neighborhood supermarket on Davidson one day not much later. We were having fun when the attendant made us stop. On our way out of the lot a lady asked us to help her with her groceries. After taking her things to her car and unloading it for her she gave us some money, just enough for the candy we wanted to buy.

Before I could put the money in my pocket and begin the walk to the candy store, Greg pulled at my arm to get my attention the way he always did. I stopped impatiently and looked down into his eyes.

"Hey, let's do this again!" he said.

"Do what?" I asked.

"Let's help another lady with her groceries and get some more money," he said simply. If I had known as much about the Bible as my mother I probably would have said something like "Out of the mouths of babes..." Instead I was just a stupid young boy talking to his little brother whom I thought was more stupid than I was.

"Okay," I said while still headed to the candy store. "We'll hustle up some more money right after we get the candy or maybe we'll do it this afternoon."

"Okay, Okay..." Greg said following me like he always did as I headed off. "But we'd get a lot more money if we stayed here and hustled while it's crowded instead of buying candy."

The strength of his reasoning gripped me much tighter than his little hand which was again clutching my sleeve. But I was cool.

"Well... I guess we can get a few more before we leave," I said in a premeditated, calm fashion, releasing the money in my pocket and slowly scratching my chin. I snatched a quick glance down at Greg to see if he looked as if he knew how right he was. He did. He was already pointing to the cars that were lined up to get into the lot of the supermarket. We were the only kids around except for kids with their parents.

My little brother and I were indeed in the position to make what was for us a small fortune. Greg did know how right he was, but he still let me be the boss and make the decision about staying and hustling. I was still the big brother, but from that point, I was not the only man in our house who was bringing in money and my mother loved it more than we did.

The money really wasn't much. But what was important, and what she tried to make us see then and there was the fact that both of her little boys were working and working together. She even talked of us going into business later on as men. She was very proud. She said it was a blessing.

Greg and I hustled together at several supermarkets after that. We didn't realize at the time, but we even diversified when we started bagging groceries and doing home deliveries. Our business, our money, and our mother's pleasure grew steadily.

We went to those games I promised Greg we would go to. We went to just about every weekend, Detroit Tiger, home game. We went, that is, whenever we thought we had the time to take off from our business. We saw fewer and fewer games. And we all but forgot about the fact that we had gone into business to buy candy. Business and making money was much sweeter.

Those were sweet times in general. That is until a recession, and then suburban shopping malls caused many supermarkets in Detroit to close. Worse still, even before the markets closed, Greg fell ill with pneumonia again. Bright afternoons of making money and going to the ballpark turned into gloomy times of listening to games at home on the radio. Punctuating the sound of the radio announcer's voice was the sound of Greg's coughing, which never seemed to stop. He coughed so hard I forgot about the game. Greg was weak and he slept a lot. Whenever he woke up and asked about the score of the games, I sometimes couldn't even tell him who was playing, let alone the score.

My mother prayed and nursed Greg. We all did in fact. Greg seemed to sense that his illness was infecting the rest of the family with a terrible gloom and he fought as hard as he could to recover. But our business partnership had ended forever.

Chapter 7

ANOTHER NIGHTMARE

I can only catch glimpses of my family. They are huddled close by in a corner of a room in my father's house. They are trying to help me. Oh it hurts. It hurts so much. But my family cannot help me. They call out to me. They cry out to me. But they cannot help. They have been in the storm and I now am in the storm—a blizzard of slaps and punches. I am eight years old and I am back in the storm.

The noxious, alcoholic wind of my father's breath burns my nose. An instant later, one of his punches smashes into my nose with a crunch. My nose closes. I can feel blood seeping out. Then he punches me again and I feel nothing. Pictures of my family sweep by me as my father's punches knock me back and forth and then start to turn me almost all the way around. Then one of the punches closes one of my eyes. Half my view of my family is cut off.

I look up. The single light above my father's head casts a shadow on his face. More punches. His blows explode on my face and body. He beats me against another wall. I look up again. I can see his face now. It looks like the face of Greg. It's Greg's face, older, snarling, and with more lines, but it's Greg's face... No, no Greg would never beat me like this.

More punches. My body slams into a table and then into another wall. I look up to my father's face again. His face is hooded in the shadow again, like the hood of an executioner. My mother calls out for my father to have mercy in God's name. But now, in this space, my father is God, or rather the devil, and I am in hell. My mother calls out to him again. Oh, why did she ever let him back in? Why didn't some of her scripture-learned wisdom make her smarter about this monster of a man? She calls out his name again, begging for mercy for me. But he doesn't answer.

Finally the beating stops, but not the hurting and terrible aching. As the sharp pains give way to numbness there is my family, only a few yards away, but still unable to touch me because my father remains between them and me. He tells them to keep away from me. He says he's not through. That is part of his punishment, to make you wait for pain, to make you wait to see if there will be more pain, and to make you beg and pray to him for mercy.

I can see again. I have to squint through my swollen eyelids, but I can see my family again. It is a terrible family portrait. They are all clinging to one another, crying, and moaning for me. Their hands reach out in my direction, but they do not move toward me.

My father stands between us sweating, scowling, and almost exhausted from the effort of beating me, and from the alcohol that infects and pollutes his blood.

My family is still there, still huddled in the corner, still begging my father not to hit me anymore. He staggers but still stays between them and me. He tells them to keep away. He slumps against the wall as if to fall. They sense he is collapsing and they move toward me. My aching head swivels "no" above my throat which is clogged with mucous, blood, and sucked-up tears. Dazed, I wave my hand and shake my head again as my family tries to approach me. We all look at my father. He is winning the battle to stay on his feet. His body slumped against the wall. His hands clutch the wall and make their way up. One after the other his hands grope upward. They grasp nothing but somehow his hands rise upon the wall and soon he is almost erect.

He stands there looking at me, puffing breath that reeks of alcohol and vomit. In the deathly coldness of that room, his breath forms billowy, gaseous clouds. With his burning blood-shot eyes, and long, crooked teeth he looks like a dragon. The clouds of breath grow larger as he tries to summon strength. I look at my family. Not even the slightest trace of mist escapes from their mouths—frozen in their fear, they barely breath.

My family retreats, helpless, sobbing, and intertwined, they gaze across the abyss of my father's presence at me in silence.

Chapter 8

BAD BOY

I was eleven years old the first time that I committed a crime. The crime was theft.

I wanted candy, so I stole it from a neighborhood candy store.

I had sized the place up for a long time by buying candy there and watching the routine of the shopkeeper. It was just a matter of waiting until his back was turned long enough (like when he was busy with a customer who was buying a lot of things) and snatching the candy I wanted and then stuffing it in my pocket. I even figured that I'd hang around and buy a little something so as to cover my tracks. Why should I run? If I ran, then the storekeeper would know something was up even if he didn't miss the candy. He might follow me and find the candy. Or even if he didn't do that, he would certainly be watching after that.

But that day was the day when I really began stumbling and bumbling my way into crime and toward prison.

First, I remember how scared I was and how much I wanted that candy. These were the two things that were certainly weighing in the balance in my young mind— my fear and my desire. I didn't ponder ramifications or consequences, no kid headed for trouble ever does. Immediate fear and desire were the only things I had in mind.

I was just about to call the whole thing off and just buy some candy and leave the store when something odd occurred to me. I remembered what must have been my first candy caper about four years before the time I stood in the store. This was the time when my brother Greg and I had stolen from God and gotten away with it. It was one Sunday morning in church. Greg and I had been given some money to put into the collection plate by our grandmother who had stayed home from church that Sunday to nurse our half-sister Barbara who was sick.

It was just me and Greg, and we sat there in church quietly dressed in the best clothes we had. Even while listening to all that powerful and beautiful music all we could think about was candy—candy, candy, and more candy. Even in the midst of all that was holy we sat there mouthing the words to songs about heaven and redemption while literally salivating about candy.

We never spoke about what was then the unspeakable: Stealing from God. We had the money right in our pockets, all ready to be spent. We each fondled our small change while we watched the shiny brass collection plate approaching us as it went from one hand to another. The plate would come to me first and then I would pass it to Greg. I was absolutely sure that Greg would do whatever I did and so thereafter it was all up to me.

By the time the plate came to me I had an empty little fist suspended above it. I took the plate with one hand, faked a deposit into the plate by barely opening the fist. Then I passed the plate quickly to Greg.

That's when he really surprised me. Greg had his money in his hand all along. Despite wanting candy, he had intended to put his money in the plate. When he saw what I did, he stuffed the money back into his pocket and *then* faked putting the money into the plate by doing the worst possible imitation of my example.

I expected to be kicked right down to hell by God at that very moment or maybe snatched down there by the devil. But nothing happened. No one had noticed what we had done. In the process of and the midst of all that music and clapping and shouting to God, no one had noticed our little crime. Greg's hesitation was the only hitch.

We bought candy for days with that money. And we, of course, lied to our grandmother about making the offering.

We never stole from the collection plate again though. It wasn't because we reformed ourselves. The reason was that as far as I can remember our grandmother never missed another Sunday of church.

Four years later, that memory of "stealing from God" without being punished was the tiny event that tipped the scales that balanced fear and desire in my mind, in favor of desire.

I watched until the merchant had turned his back, then I went for the candy. I took a piece and was about to stroll out of the store. Then, as I remember, the phone rang in the back of the store and the merchant disappeared in the back to answer it. Now there was even more time to steal and still much more candy to take. It seemed silly to take just one piece for Greg and me. "Why not get more?" I thought to myself while making sure that the storekeeper was still not in the front of the store. "More for later and more for others. Why not get as much as I could so that I would never have to steal any candy again?" I stuffed my pockets and started to leave. Before leaving, I looked once again toward the back of the store. The merchant was still somewhere in the back. I could have gotten even more candy and, shit, even robbed the place I thought to myself as I walked to the doorway.

Before I could get there a cop appeared.

"That's him, officer!" A voice from the back of the store said. "That's the kid I called in about."

The cop, who was white and well over six feet, looked down on me with an expression that was half-frowning and half-smiling.

"Who? This little guy?..." The officer said. "He's part of the gang that's been holding you up?"

"Na... No! No sir! Not me!" I exclaimed.

"Well, he's certainly been stealing from me... check his pockets." The storekeeper said as he finally came out of the back of the store. "I've been watching the little thief from the back for about five minutes. Even before I went back there to answer the phone I knew he was up to something. He was standing around and staring trying to throw me off by making me think that his mind was a million miles away—but I knew that his mind was on stealing from me."

Then the cop sort of smiled and then *asked* not ordered me to take out what I had in my pockets.

On the way home in the squad car the cop asked me a lot of questions mostly about my home life. When he asked if my father lived with us and I paused and then said "no," he stopped asking questions.

My aunt Loretta, who was sitting for us while Mama was at work, started crying as soon as she saw us coming up the walk. The cop tried to console my aunt by telling her that boys like me often do "little" things like I had done, that don't amount to much of anything in the long run if they're handled right. He said that he and his brothers and sisters were raised by his mother, and he and his brothers had been a lot worse than me and Greg when they were our ages. This took a lot of weight off of me. I felt relieved.

I listened to both of them talk about how hard it was to raise kids (the cop had three of his own) and how television and the lack of Christian principles were going to ruin the generation that was growing up at that time. The cop seemed very friendly and not nearly as stern as I had heard cops were.

My father was never mentioned, but it was clear that he was the unspoken topic. They talked about "kids needing more strictness and guidance." In my own mind, I even agreed. I was just so happy my mother hadn't yelled at me or beat me for stealing that I would have been the first to proclaim my own guilt, as well as renounce Satan, as long as my penitence did not include a beating.

As my aunt and the cop talked on and on, I was

thinking about crime. I concluded that the big thing was not getting caught. In the absence of a good ass whipping, which was just what I deserved, getting caught was the only mistake that I could see that I had made in my then fledgling criminal career. The balance between fear and desire had been decisively upset in favor of desire. I was now afraid of nothing.

Instead of feeling sorry for what I had done, I started to replay the whole incident in my mind, and I tried to note all the mistakes I had made so as to fashion a perfect crime in my mind—for future reference.

Looking back, I realize that had my father been in the home at the time of this incident, I would have certainly been beaten and beaten badly. But I also understand now that it probably would have done little or no good. The reason being that my father resorted to mental and physical abuse in response to just about anything that upset him, especially when he was drunk. His indiscriminate abuse taught us nothing. I did not learn to fear the consequences of specific kinds of behavior, but just to be afraid. But to them (in this time, decades before talk shows), a firm hand seemed better to the cop and my mother than no hand at all.

The cop finally left and things around the house started to settle down a bit. My aunt Loretta and my sisters returned to the laundry. Greg watched some cowboy show on TV like Wyatt Earp or Maverick until he fell asleep, and I was sent to bed with no supper and no TV as punishment for stealing the candy.

I remember laying in bed sucking on some candy that the cop had given me. Some candy that he had presumably paid for and given to me and the other kids so that we wouldn't feel so nervous. He also told me that I should eat the candy he was giving me with the thought that I should never again steal anything and make my mother's life more difficult with that kind of trouble.

But as I lay there, I was already planning my next crime. It was a small one, of course, another candy store. This crime stuff wasn't so bad after all, I thought. At least if the punishment wasn't more than I had "suffered." There I was with a sweet taste in my mouth, with more

nerve than I'd ever felt in my life, and best of all, my little
behind I was laying on had not been touched thanks to
that wonderful cop who had brought me home.

I think I had just fallen asleep only for a few minutes
when the sound of a car pulling into the driveway awoke
me. The sound of a car struck terror in my heart because
the only person who ever parked there was my father
when he came for one of his unannounced and (hopefully)
infrequent visits.

A moment after the car door slammed, I sprang from
the bed, rushed to the window, and looked out to the
driveway to see, not my father's old beat up car, but a
fairly new car, and one that I had not seen in the driveway
before.

Whoever had driven up was soon knocking at the door.

Through the crack in the door of the room my siblings
and I slept in, I saw my mother go to the door and open
it. The smell of liquor swept into the house when she
opened the door, but I knew by the kind tone in my
mother's voice that it was not my father that she was
talking to.

She stayed at the door for several moments, never
letting the person who stood there in. Then her voice
changed, and I heard a strangely familiar voice... it was
the cop's voice. He was pleading to my mother to let him
in so that she and he could have a drink. My mother
slammed the door in his face. I ran back to the bed and
jumped in and pulled the covers over me.

The cop made his way back to his car in the driveway
shouting and cursing all the way. "You just better keep
that little black bastard's nose clean. If I catch him stealing
out here again I'll beat his ass so bad he'll wish he was
dead... and so bad you won't recognize him!"

Later that night my mother sat on the side of the bed
and told me, "Ya see son, ya can't trust anyone." With
the exception of her I didn't trust anyone. So I agreed
with that. Then she said: "Nothing good ever comes from
wrong doing." The cop's angry threats had scared me a
little, but I still had the sweet taste of candy in my mouth.
So I wondered, as I looked into my mother's dark and
serious eyes, if in fact she was right about that.

Chapter 9

ANCHORS AWAY

I have much to both thank and condemn the United States of America for, though I think the things that I condemn this country for, have been and will be more or less self-evident throughout the course of this book. But the things for which I am thankful deserve highlighting and emphasis. This is because I consider myself nothing less than a loyal citizen of the United States and a patriot.

But unlike Nathan Hale (who is quoted as saying: "I only regret that I have but one life to live for my country."), I don't want *another* life to live for this country, I just want a chance to live the life I've already been given after I've settled my outstanding debt to society. With hard work, clean living, and the grace of God, that chance that my family and I are all praying for will come my way.

One debt of gratitude that I owe to this country is for giving me the joy of being able to give my mother what she herself called the proudest day of her life.

In 1975, I was seventeen. Detroit was in the deepening throws of a great, local recession. President Nixon was into the third year of his second term. Mercifully, he had ended the Vietnam War, but his detrimental urban policies were in full effect. Young black men were coming home from Vietnam, but they were returning to desolation.

People who had the resources to move were moving to the south or to the west or to the suburbs. My family was trapped. Detroit was becoming an economic ghost town. Moreover, the fastest growing segment of the population was drug-addicted zombies. Many of the young black men in this category were Vietnam vets who had become hooked on heroin, marijuana, and LSD in the war they had fought, and Nixon said they'd won.

Even though scores of black men were returning from the service to our neighborhood, the military seemed like the best place for me to be. The end of the war in Vietnam meant that the chances of getting killed were not as great as they had been, so my mother reluctantly agreed that I should try a stint in the service.

My family and my friends thought that I had fallen for the Navy recruitment propaganda when I chose that branch of the service. Sure I did want to: "Join the Navy and see the world," but I actually chose the Navy because it was the branch that President Kennedy had served in. I was six when he was killed. The only things I can clearly remember were the long lines of cars in his funeral procession on TV, and the muffled drum that beat constantly. My mother cried harder when President Kennedy was killed than when my father beat her; from that, even a six-year-old could deduce that a truly great man had been taken from this world.

Years after Kennedy was gone, my mother explained her love of him by saying that both he and Martin Luther King had stood up to the crackers in the South, and told them that their treatment of black people was both illegal and unchristian. I chose the Navy in great part to honor Kennedy, and also to please my mother.

I had some big reservations about going though. Not the least of which was the fact that it seemed my departure would be another factor in the ongoing disintegration of my family. My sister Gale had already left, my father had not been a part of the family for years (thank God), and my brother Greg's well-being, both physical and otherwise, was not assured. It was Greg and Tracey alone who would stay home with my mother.

It took a long time for me to decide to go. My mother said that it would be best for me, to at least give it a try. She said that between Greg and me, I was the most mature and could therefore get the most out of the experience. She also seemed to feel, but didn't really say, that she was very worried about Greg and his ailments, and that she wanted to be able to attend to them herself, and in the manner that had brought him along that far in life.

Another thing that made me want to go into the Navy was women. My earliest and most serious sweethearts had either moved away or gotten married, mostly to guys in the service. The idea of "a girl in every port" appealed to me. The sheer number of women a guy could find by being in the Navy seemed to me the most compelling attraction.

There was another problem with women, too. It had to do with the quality and nature of my relationships with women. Relationships just seemed to come and go like day and night; nothing seemed to last and grow. I never talked to anyone about this, not because I was the only guy that this was happening to—far from it. Every guy I knew subscribed to the 3-Fs. It seemed that "find 'em, fuck 'em, and forget 'em" was the way of the black man's world back then. I went along with it but I wanted more. I wanted someone of my own, forever. But that's not the kind of thing that you bring up when you're paling around with the 3-F club.

Don't get me wrong, I was a "Roadrunner." I was the very epitome of the kind of guy that Motown artist Junior Walker wrote and sang about. I was more or less happy with the state of affairs that existed between young black men and women of that time. I was satisfied with it, because, as a man, I was the beneficiary of the system. Men made virtually all the moves in terms of coming and going in relationships. Yes, this was a long time ago.

The reason why I never spoke to anyone about this

was because I thought at that time, I was the only guy who thought there might have been something amiss with the 3-F philosophy on relationships. I didn't want to seem like a square, but privately I wanted something that most guys didn't seem to care about. I didn't know it, but what I wanted was a family of my own.

But none of this occurred to me in this clear fashion back then. Back then it just seemed better for me to move on to whatever came next and for me to try to hold on to that which was near and dear for as long as I could. The trick was to do all of this at once. And, of course, it was impossible.

But there I stood, strong and straight on that sunny day in 1975. Dressed in my brand new, white uniform, I stood with about one thousand other Navy men and saluted the flag as it was run up the pole. This was the day that I graduated from basic training, and six weeks later, I would be put aboard the USS Lexington, an aircraft carrier.

I was in the company of Admirals, elected officials, and other brave and strong young men. My family stood with the hundreds of other families on the peer, happy, proud, and waving frantically.

The parade field was hot and humid as Company 128, my company, marched toward the captains and admirals who were in the review stands. We did fancy drills with our rifles, then stood at parade rest, as we were saluted by our superiors. I glanced up ever so carefully sideways, hoping to catch my Mama smiling proudly—as I knew she would be.

Later my mother told me how good and happy I looked on the parade field. She told me that her eyes never left me.

That image of my family together, remarkably happy, reasonably healthy, and resoundingly proud was as vivid and beautiful then, as it is painful in my memory now, because that was the last time I was ever to see them all together alive, well, and happy.

Chapter 10

THE HOMECOMING

The letters I received from my mother about how things were going were terrible. For one thing, and perhaps the worst thing, Greg was losing ground fast. He was losing ground in every imaginable way. His health was bad, and even worse than his health was his judgment. My mother wrote of the fact that Greg was not working, which was not unusual for a young man like him, and he had dropped out of school, which was not unheard of either.

The worst of it was that Greg was not even looking for work, and he was in an almost constant search for drugs. It seemed that as I sailed further and further away, things at home were getting worse and worse. Greg and Tracey were the only ones of the family living with mother—and Greg was now a drug addict. According to my mother, my sister Gale also had a drug problem. I was the one at sea, but it was my family that was sinking.

When I finally went home on leave, I could see that things were as bad as my mother had said, and in some senses worse. Greg was indeed a junkie. So was my sister.

But what my mother had not reported accurately was the fact that she herself was steadily declining. She appeared more drawn and unsteady. The house on Cherrylawn (we had moved from Tyler in 1970) that was her pride and joy was beginning to show signs of wear and tear. Although it had always been modest, it always had been clean. But now it seemed neglected, the yard unkempt, as if somehow the life had been sucked out of the house.

There were more ominous signs. Among them the fact that my mother had stopped cooking. My mother was a dietitian and a wonderful cook. We used to say that she could make tuna fish that could only be described as "the caviar of the ghetto." But she had just stopped cooking. Even more ominous were the dirty needles that lay strewn all over the basement.

The very last and perhaps the most telling sign of the decline of the home was Greg's condition. My mother could no longer care for him the way she had wanted to. She no longer had the patience or strength to keep after him. His decline reflected hers, and hers reflected his.

It had never been that way before, of course. Before, Mama had always been there to nurse Greg through his illnesses. But drugs were a sickness that even her love could not cure. Greg was virtually on his own now. My mother, when not working, mostly just stayed in bed in a state of deepening depression. I could see that Greg's use of drugs was in part his desperate way of trying to fill the void in his heart I left when I went away to the navy.

Even at our best, we were always pretty close to poverty, but this was a new level, a new low. There was no spirit in the house. There was no violence in the house, but in some ways, it was worse than when we lived with my father. At least then, there was some sense or feeling that there was in fact a better place for us to be.

My mother attributed this malaise to the fact that I had left. She told me, while I was on leave, about a year after I enlisted, that she wanted me to come back home. I said that I would come. But I didn't agree with her theory. To me, the gloom in the house was tied to the poor health of my mother and to Greg and his addiction. I had no idea what I could do about either one of those problems.

In a way, I didn't want to come home. I hadn't achieved any of the things that I had left home to accomplish. I had found no training that I could use in civilian life, and although I had met a lot of women, nothing lasted, and nothing made me feel loved. The same old Pussy Posses that military life was famous for were no longer much fun.

Coming home after my hitch was over, the way my mother suggested, would not solve any of these problems, but it was what she wanted, and so I said that I would drop out of the Navy before my four-year hitch ended. Back on the ship, I worked as a boiler technician, helping out in the armory every now and then, and I bided my time. I didn't have long to wait.

About a month after my last trip home on leave, I received word from the naval chaplain that Greg had been murdered.

In a way, I was prepared for it—though what I had expected to hear about was an overdose. The last time I had seen Greg, his very essence had gone. All the boyishness and innocence had deserted him. But he had rallied when he saw me. Something came out of nowhere and made him seem stronger. He promised that he'd try to get help and try to take better care of himself and our mother. I knew he didn't mean it, but still I loved him dearly for at least trying to make me feel better.

When I went home for Greg's funeral, it was not like it had been on those earlier trips home on leave. My sisters were there with me, but Greg was gone. And his so-called best friend was walking around like nothing had happened. This was the guy who had murdered Greg. I knew the guy, and I couldn't believe that he would have blown a hole in my brother's chest with a twelve-gauge shotgun and then leave him for dead in a filthy alley.

I buried Greg, but I could not bury my rage which was inspired by Greg's friend's betrayal. I went back to my ship after Greg's funeral. When I returned about three weeks later, I had enough explosives with me to destroy half a city block.

One evening, I dressed in military fatigues, left my mother at home staring at our television set and slung a backpack full of explosives over my shoulder.

I trudged through the rain to the home of the guy who had murdered Greg. I hid in the alley and unpacked the explosives. As the rain poured over me, I attached a small but powerful device to the side of the house. I crouched down and waited there with the switch in my hand.

The rain poured down and soaked through my clothes to my skin. More than an hour passed. The empty driveway, in clear view from where I was positioned, meant that my quarry was not home yet. So I continued to wait.

At first, I was going to set the timer so as to give myself enough time to leave. But then I wondered, why leave at all? When the charge of explosives I had prepared went off, I would be as dead as the guy I was going to blow up. I was better off dead because I was going to be caught. There was no way around it. The explosives that I had taken from the armory of the ship would be eventually missed, and soon after that the explosives would be traced to me. I knew all this and I still didn't care. My brother was dead. My mother was very ill. The rest of my family had scattered again after my brother's funeral. I no longer had a family. I had no education, no training other than the kind that would soon end my life, and the life of the guy who had practically killed my brother. I had nothing.

Rain continued to pour over me, and I sat there, until finally a car pulled into the driveway. My brother's *best friend* got out of the car and ran quickly inside to avoid the downpour. I got everything ready. I decided to not use the timer. There was no way back. Or so I thought. Not only would the explosives be missed but they might *already* have been missed. In that case, the theft would already have been traced to me. I got ready to die.

Then a baby cried inside the house. For the first time, I thought about the other people in the house. How many more were in there? How many more lives would I be ending in addition to Greg's supposed friend and mine? Who would take care of my mother, and how much would learning about both my suicide and murder shorten her life?

I must have sat there for another half-hour, just thinking, and listening to the rain, before disconnecting the charges from the detonator and walking home through the rain. Tears flowed freely down my face, mixing with the raindrops that had already fallen there.

Gregory

He was so kind,
a Black boy, just confused.
He never hurt anyone,
yet he was born to lose.
Big doe eyes,
curly black hair,
and skin like smooth
butter.
Blessed with an uncanny
ability to love everybody.
Even the best friend
who caused him to
meet his end.
A gaping hole,
where his heart
used to be!!!
A SCREAM!!!
Run, Gregory, run...
The ALLEY!
So dark...
...run Gregory.
Don't let the rats
get you!!!
"MAMA!!! MAMA!!!"
RUN GREGORY!!!
Knock! KNOCK HARDER!!!
Another SCREAM!!!
"MAMA!"
"HE SHOT ME"
Make it to Mama's
bed.
"it hurts..."
"Mama, it hurts..."
Big doe eyes

losing life,
taken maliciously
by another
Greg was my best friend.
He was my BROTHER!
So young,
so trusting.
So...
SO DEAD!!!

Though the charges had been disconnected, and the detonator and the timer placed neatly back in the pack that bounced on my shoulder, somewhere within me a fuse was still lit. And somewhere within me an explosive charge of rage as volatile and powerful as any stick of dynamite still waited to be set off.

I resolved in my mind that I didn't care if the explosives were missed back on the ship. "Some mother fuckin' rat is going to get his ass blown up tonight." I said out loud as I turned and retraced my steps back in the direction of the place that I had just left.

I got more and more mad as I walked back much faster than I had walked away.

"Shit..." I said once again out loud to no one but myself and the rain. "My God Damn brother is DEAD! Stone cold DEAD!... At least one rat in this world is going to die tonight!"

Then I started to run. I reached the house where Greg's so-called friend lived. I glanced at it and kept running. I never even broke my stride.

I just kept on running until I found what I was looking for.

About thirty minutes later I stood at the edge of a large and nearly vacant lot. I stood there and looked at the rundown, abandoned apartment building that was near the center of the lot.

The abandoned building blew up right on schedule. The flash illuminated acres of vacant lots in that section of the city. A red and gold cloud spiraled upward through relentless sheets of pouring rain and to the low, flat, starless night sky.

The flash died out as quickly as it had been born. But at ground level, a fire had started. Debris from the explosion, blown into the air, began falling back to earth.

I didn't realize it then, but the explosion was an expression of my rage. And looking back, I suppose I'd like to think that the fire symbolized a funeral pyre in honor of my dead brother. After all, he had died as a P.O.W. in the great drug war that was being waged against American society.

The police- and fire-department sirens sounded in the distance, but I didn't walk or run away. I stayed to get my final satisfaction.

I stood there watching until I saw rats scampering away from the flames. That's when I knew that at least *one* rat had been blown to hell that night in Detroit. That's when I finally walked away.

Chapter 11

NO PARTICULAR PLACE TO GO

February, 1977, I went back to my ship tired, lonely, and with no sense of direction. I spent most of my time on the empty flight deck looking out at the Gulf of Mexico, wondering where my life was headed and how deeper I would dig into depression.

It was possible that if I had sought therapy upon my return to the ship, I would now be two years short of retiring. But mentally, I was long gone from the Navy by then. My brother's death had taken its toll on me and the Navy granted me a hardship discharge. Soon after that I was back in Detroit living in my mother's house and desperately looking for a job—still wandering hopelessly.

Having been a member of the United States Armed Forces meant nothing if you were a poor, nineteen-year-old, black male like I was then in March of 1977.

There were virtually no jobs to be found.

I finally got a job at a golf course. I was a payroll supervisor and it was working out okay for a while. Soon the boss introduced me to his young nephew. Did you see it coming? Well, I sure didn't. Before I knew what hit me, the little, white wise-ass had my damn job, and I was back home staring at the want ads while my mother worked marathon hours at Detroit Memorial Hospital in Downtown Detroit.

This went on for weeks until one night I went out with one of my friends who was in a similar tight spot. We were just riding around, we had no particular place to go, no money. We got bored looking at the same old ghetto that we lived in day after day, so we drove over to another neighborhood, a white one.

This was a section that had nice homes, decent public services, and a lot of very good stores and shops. We started talking about how nice it must be to live there, and that if we had been brought up in a neighborhood like that, we'd still be living there. We decided that things seldom change in life for better or for worse after you're born.

After this bit of philosophizing, our talk turned back to reality and to our poverty. We had nothing. Our pockets were just about empty. The money that put the gas in the tank was borrowed.

We talked briefly about how hard it was to find work. Then we looked around at the clean streets and beautiful shops. We looked at each other and then started talking about how easy it would be to rob one of the stores.

We talked so much we didn't notice the squad car that was approaching from the rear, to pull us over.

The officers from the squad car came to the sides of our car and told us to get out. They checked our licenses and scanned the inside of our car with their flashlights.

They were just about to let us go when one of the cops asked gruffly what we were doing in that particular neighborhood. I swear to God this is *exactly* what my friend said:

"Oh, we was just ridin' around lookin' at how nice everything is here and we were talkin' about maybe robbin' a few places."

The cops looked at each other for a split second. The next thing my friend and I knew we were flat against the side of the car, with our hands behind our heads.

We were arrested and charged with attempted unarmed robbery. There had been a series of robberies in that area, and they had been carried out by a pair of black men—not my friend and I—but by a pair of black men nevertheless. My friend and I were picked out of a lineup and we were convicted and sent to prison.

The year was 1977. I got two years for a crime I did not commit.

Chapter 12

IN AND OUT OF THIS WORLD

Like so many pages torn from a calendar, two years of my life were ripped from me, all for the crime of being in the wrong place, at the wrong time, and the "wrong" color.

I stayed in that hell hole of a prison for two years. The worst part of it was not the time I did. The worst part of it still stays with me until this day, and will remain with me until the day I die. And that was the fact that my first child entered this world while I was serving this unjust sentence.

The year was 1978. I remember the first day her mother, Linda, brought my daughter to the prison so I could see her. Her mother and I had named her Arlinda, which is a combination of Linda's and my name. She was so beautiful. So tiny and so beautiful. I cried when I first held her. I felt like I was such a failure. I had nothing to offer her—not even myself.

I fell into a depression.

At night I lay awake in my cell and listened to the

constant din and chatter in the prison. It was maddening.

There was laughter, screams of anguish, singing, story telling... everything humanly and inhumanely imaginable could be heard in that prison. It continued unabated until the lights went out.

After lights out, there were still intermittent screams and fits of yelling. A lot of the guys in there clearly had mental problems and should have been somewhere else.

One of the most frightening things to hear in prison are fights. You can not only hear the shouting, screaming, the grunts and groans, but you can also hear the kicks and punches, and blows from blunt instruments. You could hear those things, that is, if the noise from the cheering inmates wasn't too loud.

At night I'd just lie in the bunk of my cell and try to shut everything out. I'd lie there staring out the window at the outside world.

One of my earliest cellmates was really deranged by free-world standards. Even by prison standards he was considered eccentric. For several weeks I shared a bunk with this guy who caught rats for sport. I think you know how I feel about rats.

The guy would take peanut butter from the prison dining hall and build his own traps for the rats. He'd catch them, then *keep* some of them there in the cell with us in boxes that he called "their cages." If I threw them out, days later, he'd have more to replace the one's I had evicted. I never felt safe, sleeping with those rats.

But eventually I did get some peace and quiet in my cell. The inmate who caught the rats was moved and I got a decent fellow, one I could talk to. But we communicated so well that my mind rushed back to the outside world—not the dismal world that I just left, but the one further back in time. The world in which Greg and I had lived as boys and teenagers. After talking to my new cellmate about sports, I'd remember things like how Greg and I used to star as running backs in the community football league. With Greg blocking for me, I remember carrying defenders on my back for yards at a time, all the way to the goal line, as I scored touchdown after touchdown.

The memory was a sweet one, but the feeling always turned sad and bitter. Invariably, after each heroic touchdown I relived, the daydream would be shattered by the noise of the prison, or worse still, it would be ruined by the memory of something like Greg's illness, or his drug-use, or his death. Nothing seemed to be able to ease my painful past.

To say that the noise in prison is maddening is no overstatement. The constant din makes you forget about the act of listening. It gets to the point that you don't listen well even in the absence of noise. My mother, who came to visit me then often, said that my mind seemed to be elsewhere, and that I didn't seem to hear her.

Sometimes my mind was indeed elsewhere, thinking about some pleasing or painful daydream while she was trying to communicate. But more often than not, when the words of visitors were unable to get through to me, the reason was that the din of the prison environment was still ringing in my ear, even in the comparatively quiet visitors area.

Sometimes it would be literally hours after lights out in that prison before I could even begin to hear myself think. For weeks I didn't realize this, and I'd fall asleep without ever having heard myself think all day.

But then one starry, moonlit night, I resolved to just stay awake and look out to the night sky beyond the bars on my windows.

A couple of hours after lights out, things really began to quiet down. Soon it was almost completely quiet. Only an occasional slamming hallway door or the footsteps of a guard on patrol broke the silence.

For the first time I heard the sounds of nature outside—crickets and owls for instance. Then, for the first time since I was in prison, I heard the wind. It was beautiful and it seemed to speak to me. It told me what I already knew. It told me that the noise of the prison was costing me my peace of mind and perhaps my mind itself.

That same night that I heard the wind, the light of the moon filled my cell. Only the shadow of the window's bars that fell starkly on the floor spoiled the beauty of the light. I looked out and I looked up and I had hope.

I remember that night well. And I savored peaceful times like that, whenever I got them, for the rest of my days in prison.

I remember that I looked at clouds floating freely across the moon that night. It was so quiet and so clear that I listened in that God-sent silence wondering if those clouds crossing the moon would make any sound. For if they had made even the slightest sound, I would have surely heard it in that almost perfect silence.

It was almost religious. If my mother had been there, she would have said I was experiencing the peace that surpasses all understanding. I longed for it and I hungered for it to last. I didn't even want to sleep. The conscious experience of this peacefulness was better than any dream I had experienced or could imagine, and more invigorating and restful than the best night's sleep I had ever had.

Chapter 13

TRYING TO START OVER

I got out of prison for the crime I did not commit in 1979. I sincerely tried to put the injustice that had been perpetrated against me behind me. This attempt was my first failure after leaving prison and the beginning of an unfortunate pattern that was to continue.

The issue of having been innocent always stuck in my mind. It was never a crutch to lean on, an excuse for later failures, but it did become a club with which I inflicted pain on others and myself.

One of the first things that I did when I left prison that year was to marry my daughter's mother. I tried to make it work and so did she, but we were not successful. Other than poverty, the only thing that we had in common was our love for Arlinda, our child. Anyone who has ever tried to raise even the smallest of families in the best of economic circumstances will tell you that that is not enough.

In 1981, my son Omar was born. I was not a proud

father. Omar was a beautiful baby boy and I was proud of *him*, but I was not proud of myself. I was already a failure as a provider for the family that I had before Omar. Now there was yet another reminder, Omar, that said as loudly with his presence, as he did with his crying, that I was failing again.

I tried to find work and did. But the jobs never seemed to last long enough to keep us out of soup kitchens. The last job I had before I took up crime was in a chemical plant.

Talk about crime. The working conditions in that "plant" were criminal. I'm sure that if the place existed today it would be fined out of existence by the OSHA (The Occupational Health and Safety Administration). Suffice it to say that my job, along with that of several other blacks, was to clean up toxic waste that no one (white) wanted to go near.

But as bad as that was, I would have stuck with the job, low pay and all. But just like always, I was laid off. It was like we (the blacks) were migrant workers, only in our case there was no place for us to migrate to when the season of work was over at the plant—did I say "Plant"?— well based on the low (near no) pay, the working conditions, and the way they turned us out with little or no notice, "Plant" could well have been an abbreviation, short for *plant*ation.

After that job was over, I'd had enough. I couldn't take it anymore. It was 1980. A full year after I had been released from prison had passed. I finally got the message. The message was: Nobody who has a decent job wants to give it to an ex-con. Even an ex-con who had done a stint in the Navy and had earned a hard-won GED diploma while in prison.

I knew plenty of guys who were robbing. But after my experience with the guy who told the cops that he and I were thinking about holding up a store, I decided to go it alone.

Once with no gun, and another time soon after that with a gun that had no bullets, I robbed a Coney Island and a Church's Chicken fast-food restaurant. I took in about $3,500.00 total. Mission accomplished! My kids ate, and for the first time in their lives, they ate well. And for the first time in *my* life, when a member of my family asked for more food, there was more to be had without someone else giving up theirs. I even opened bank accounts in the kids names. Things were not going well between my wife and I. But even that didn't matter to me. Finally, I was a provider.

Unfortunately, when I hopped over the counter at the Church's Chicken, I left a fingerprint.

About four months after the last robbery, I was picked up. I was swiftly tried, convicted, and put back into prison. Once again it was for a two-year stretch.

I soon found out that being in prison for something that I did do is no more satisfying than being in for something that I didn't. Prison is prison no matter how you slice it. *Nothing* makes it worthwhile being in here.

My wife stopped writing and visiting. It was the kids that I was concerned about. I no longer cared much about her. We had drifted apart well before the robberies, and once I had caught her taking drugs and having sex with another guy. And even that, I really didn't care about— except for the implications involved as far as the kids were concerned. And those implications were to prove very important later on.

But the saddest consequence of my return to prison was that my mother finally lost all hope. A letter she wrote me showed her frailty of body and spirit, and was proof to me, as if I really needed it, that when she died of lung cancer, at forty-seven years of age, with two sons dead (Bruce, her son from a previous marriage, died at the age of twenty-eight), another in prison, and two daughters scattered to the wind, she died as much as from a broken heart, as from her failed health.

One evening, during that second term in prison, I lay in my bunk on one of those special, peaceful nights. Before sleep came to me, I had a vision. I saw the soul of my mother going up into the heavens and the soul of my daughter coming down from there. From inside my prison walls, I saw their souls meet for just a moment, somewhere beyond that enormous, glowing moon, then each continued on. This vision of the unification of my daughter's descent from heaven with my mother's ascension there, helped to lift the burden of shame that I carried for years—the burden that I was in prison first when my daughter entered this world and in prison again when my mother left it.

I thanked God for bringing me this vision and for bringing me this new peace. As I was praying to him to help me find this peace again someday, I fell asleep. That kind of peace is hard to find in prison. It isn't there in fact. If it exists at all, it's inside the convict. For most of my first term in prison, it sure wasn't in me. And I had no one around me to show me the way to it. It was many months before I experienced that peace again, and even longer before I understood the source of it.

I also believe that God and my mother are looking down from heaven, leading me to something else. Something has helped me through that stretch in prison and the one that I'm serving now.

I needed what I was about to discover in prison. Much of my family was gone and the rest of it was purposely out of touch with me. There in the middle of my second stretch in prison, I was, for the first time in my life, not a part of the free world, and completely cut off from it.

Chapter 14

ONE MAN'S MEAT...

The first thing that you must realize about the experience of prison is that if you don't find some way to save yourself, you will be nothing but a piece of meat in here. That's what the system dictates. Not the administration, not the guards, but the prison system dictates that you will be kept alive here as useless, walking, dead meat until your term is completed and you're released.

Prisoners are not even in the category of cattle in the sense that their bodies have no market value. We are not even in the category of slaves, whose labor at least might be important to the economy. Other than for the prison industry which emerged over time, we the incarcerated, are of virtually no financial, economic, strategic, political, or cultural importance.

But this categorizes convicts only in terms of the prison system and those of you outside, who reside in what we call the "free world." In terms of the world in here, the world of the incarcerated, we follow our own standards.

Very often we see each other as meat. And that is as it should be. We are meat: The mind (the brain), physical strength (muscle), and manhood (our penises). The struggle is to keep control of these meats, if you will, and the struggle goes on constantly.

It has little to do with sex, physical prowess, or mental ability. Because in the world of the incarcerated, the mind, the penis, the brain, and the muscle are all metaphors for force and power, nothing more. That is all that matters in here. It's the same thing that ruled my father's house—Might makes right, might makes wrong, might makes everything.

It's good to be liked and admired and even revered, but it's safest to be feared. And safety is the most important thing in prison. It is more important than health. Poor health may kill you over time but bad personal security is sudden death.

It's all about power. Things that look like romance, sex, even friendship are most often related to power and the threat of death. That's what I mean about safety—staying alive. That's what I mean about fear. "Fear" here does not mean the fear of being hurt or losing property, in here, the only real fear is the fear of death. It is all about power.

Take sex for instance. A big thing is made about homosexuality in prison. Studies and stories have been written for generations about how pervasive it is. Let me tell you something. In here, the amount of homosexuality is probably no greater than it is on the outside. I say that for two reasons. First of all, no one who is homosexual coming into prison stays in the closet, because there *is* no closet in here. There is no closet, because people who are gay have no reason to hide it.

The pretenses and trappings of the free world do not apply in here. There are no families, no children, and nobody much cares about gender. Why should they care? We're all males in here, even the ones who've had operations. Therefore, unless you come across a horny female guard, you can forget about heterosexuality for the balance of your sentence.

With that in mind, you have to decide whether or not

VERNON REGIONAL
JUNIOR COLLEGE LIBRARY

you are going to forget about sex. Most men don't ever forget about it, and they don't stop doing it either. So at that point, the choices for straight, new men like me are few but critical. For the guys already in prison, the only questions are whether or not they want to fuck you, and if so, whether you might be able to stop them.

Notice that at this point I am no longer distinguishing between gay and straight. That is because there is no distinction. Gender in all but the clinical sense disappears behind bars. And so do labels of free-world sexual orientation. We have our own terms in here. A homosexual person who would be called a faggot in the free world would be called a "girl" or "woman" in here. A person who is desired as a sex object (forget about being a partner) would be simply a "hole." A person who can be exploited sexually or otherwise is called a "punk." And a guy who belongs to another person because that person has "taken" him is "so and so's bitch or punk."

Coming into prison I was what you would call homophobic. I guess you would say that I came hating gays the way most straight men have been taught and trained by the free world society. I always thought for one thing that they, the gays, were weak and stupid and inherently inferior to straight men. Well, behind bars, stereotypes do not always hold together. In this, the world of the incarcerated "Women" can be and often are just as aggressive and powerful as any straight man.

Before I came to a confrontation with this prison reality, I was involved in a brief incident which did nothing but reinforce the stereotypes most heterosexual men harbor. I had just been imprisoned for my first armed robbery. I considered myself "bad," in the sense of being tough—as tough as any dude in the joint—and I believed this so strongly that I felt I exuded power and not-to-be-fucked-withness. Consequently, my ego was a little bruised when I was hit on by a gay man in the hallway one day. After licking his lips at me, he approached me and asked if he could give me a blow job. I immediately hauled off and smacked him. Urged on by other convicts who soon gathered around, I finished him off with a few more punches and finally a few kicks.

"No faggot is going to mess with me!" I said as I looked down on the guy, feeling invincible, but I thought that it was strange that some of the same guys that had urged me on in the fight (though it was no contest really) shook their heads and smirked as they walked away—some even laughed. They knew something I didn't, something I was soon to learn. Thank God I didn't have to learn it the hard way.

I remember it was one day soon after, early in the term of my first incarceration, I was coming around the bend of a shower area. I was still toweling off and thinking about something which I have long since forgotten. I rounded the corner of the stall and ran right smack dab into some prison reality.

There in front of me was an enormous black man. I mean he was about six foot six and three hundred pounds. This guy had about a foot of his hard, black penis inserted in the anus of a young, white convict.

At first, the image struck me as grotesquely absurd—almost funny. It was like watching a Great Dane trying to mount a miniature Poodle. Yes, it was almost funny, almost...

His black hulk glistened brightly even through the dull, gray steam of the shower room. Coiled beneath him was the kid's shuddering body. It was barely visible. The black convict thrust faster and faster inside the white kid. Then I noticed blood trickling down the thin, quivering legs of the kid, and suddenly, the image was no longer funny. I had to fight to keep the food in my stomach.

Other convicts came by. Most just glanced and kept walking—evidently having seen this before. Some convicts watched and provided a comic chorus of chants like "Bust that little white ass open..." or "Make your dick come out of his mouth!"

At twenty-two, I thought I was capable of handling myself, thought I was pretty tough—I thought maybe I should do something to help this kid. But then, through the steam, I saw his face. His expression was not one of fear, or horror, but almost of... gratitude. Then I saw his hand move up to his own penis and begin to stroke it in rhythm of the black convicts thrusts.

The black convict let out a loud grunt that echoed off the cracked tiles of the shower pavilion. Then, noticing me for the first time, he looked directly at me and smiled. Violence, rape, murder, power, pleasure—it was all there in that smile. Right then I realized it would take every ounce of strength I had to survive and stay sane in that insane, prison hell. It was suddenly clear to me that if I didn't become categorically stronger than both those men, then for sure I would become one of them.

Then, the enormous, black convict extracted himself from the white kid, pushing him to the floor of the shower room as casually as he would have discarded a towel. Then, he disappeared into the steam like a magician's final trick, one that leaves his audience in awe and wonder at what they had just witnessed.

The other convicts applauded and taunted the kid who still lay on the floor. "You didn't even get a chance to come did you, white meat?" One of them jeered as he and the rest strolled away, involved in half-hearted butt pinching, towel snapping, and laughter.

Chapter 15

GYMNASIUMS FOR THE BODY AND THE MIND

I was never what you would call a fitness freak. Fortunately, I, unlike my brother Greg, was gifted with an essentially strong and healthy body. Today I stand six foot two inches and weigh a muscular and well-proportioned 220 pounds.

In terms of the muscles and the proportions, I didn't get this way and I won't stay this way by any accident.

Remember I told you that behind bars, men are little more than meat. Well, to stay safe you better be tough meat. That's why I found my way to the gymnasium.

Nobody is rich in prison and intelligence counts for relatively little. What impresses people in here are largely the same things that scare them: strength, the willingness to hurt or to kill and the willingness to die. You've got to have at least one of these things to stay alive in prison and I, like a lot of guys, choose to have strength.

With me, it's not a macho thing. And it's not a sexual thing either. I am strictly heterosexual and I don't want anything going into my anus other than toilet paper. Physical strength is a matter of survival for me.

In the gymnasium, like just about everywhere else in prison, there's noise. There's lots of it. But there's also sweat, blood, grunts, groans and work.

When I'm hitting the heavy bag or working the midsection of a sparing partner, I don't hear the guy who's fifteen feet away from me skipping rope. Nor can I hear the guy, who might be even closer, grunting his lungs out while he's pressing a few hundred pounds. Everything around me, the sounds, the sights and the smells recede below the threshold of my awareness and stay there until my own concentration is broken.

Just counting your push-ups or your sit-ups can block out everything. So does taking and giving punches in the ring. I've seen men fight entire boxing matches (as many as ten or twelve rounds) with broken ribs and never even feel anything until hours later. Things like that go beyond even strength; there's a mental focus achieved at these levels of exertion that most men in or out of prison never achieve. And guys love it.

Guys will curl bar bells for hours longer than is necessary to achieve and maintain the biceps that they have. Why do they do this? Not just for the way it makes them look, not just for how strong it makes them, but because of the way it makes them feel. I know because I love the feeling.

But the appearance of strength and power in prison is important. I'm a thinker and a writer, not a brutalizer and a fighter. And that can be a limitation in prison. Fellow inmates must be sure that you are strong, otherwise you will be exploited, without exception.

Even if you look strong and fit enough, it must also be clear that you are willing to use your strength when needed. Your physical condition can be seen with the naked eye—your toughness cannot be seen. And so you inevitably will be tested.

It's not like you see in the movies where some poor young guy, who's portrayed as being innocent anyway, comes into jail and is immediately set upon by the worst bullies in the place. In reality, it's more subtle, at least on the surface. In a real prison anyone and everyone is sized up. The predators in prison, and there are many, want to know what you might have that they might want, and how hard or easy it would be to get it from you.

Many of the rest of the people in prison are just like me. Just doing their time with hopes of some kind of life after prison.

In addition to the predators and the guys just putting in their time, you have an assortment of characters who are clearly not designed for anything other than prison. It's not that these guys are unfit for the free world in the sense that they are habitual criminals, but rather they've been in so long they can't or won't understand or relate to any other life. To me, these guys are the most frightening. These are the guys I most fear becoming like because of the extreme length of my sentence. I first noticed them when the separation from my family began, because none of these men had strong family ties.

These types are not to be confused with the crazies. Craziness though, like strength, provides some personal security. Nobody bothers the crazies or the psychos or the weirdos—they are the untouchables in prison. Guys like the roommate I had who caught the rats are not to be messed with and seldom are.

The gymnasium is a vital part of what has kept me as free as I can be within the confines of prison. But it is only a part. The other is purely mental, but like its physical counterpart, it involves training and vigorous exercise. The other places that have been so important to me are the library and the classroom, what you could call the gymnasiums of the mind.

When I was studying for my GED, I found that the classroom and the library were two of the quietest places in the prison. That's what initially drew me to education and reading. Eventually, I came to appreciate the intrinsic value of both those pursuits, but what first attracted me was the peace and quiet that I found, particularly in the library.

Not only could I hear myself think in the library, but I could also mentally: sing, dance, fight, gamble, make love, or anything else within the realm of my and the author's imagination. If someone could write it, then I could share it with him or her no matter what the experience or the situation was.

Why I didn't ever catch on to reading and learning when I was in school is a good question. The answer is that the school system which I failed in, and which failed me, in my youth was worse than what I found in prison. The class size in public school was anywhere from two to three times greater than what I found in prison. The books in prison were better and so were the teachers.

The teachers in prison were younger and usually more intellectually aggressive. Public school teachers seemed more interested in just passing students on to the next grade and keeping order (with sometimes more than forty students in a class, who could blame them). The often younger and/or more idealistic teachers in prison wanted to *see* a positive change in you. They saw convicts as a real challenge. And as products of an extremely poor school system, we were indeed a challenge to their skills, knowledge, and patience.

I got my GED during my first stretch and my associate degree during my current sentence. All along the way, in each of the dozen or so institutions that I've been in, libraries have been my greatest sanctuary. Even more so than school. This is because classes for credit were not always available, whereas libraries always were. Also as good as the teachers were, nothing compared with the freedom that I got in the libraries.

Books became like food and I became very greedy. For a while there, I became mentally fat and intellectually bloated. I'd go around spouting and spewing facts like so much regurgitated knowledge. I think I might have become obnoxious—clearly I turned a lot of guys off who just thought that I was showing off, which I was. I was proud of what I had learned. I meant no disrespect to anyone, but clearly that impression was inferred by many.

I got back on the right track, when I was asked to be a teacher's assistant. In that role, the use of my knowledge made more sense to others who had completely misunderstood me before. It also gave me a new sense of worth, which I sorely needed in the light of not hearing from my family.

My brother Greg [right] and me, at Easter, in our cheap, scratchy, and wooly suit coats.

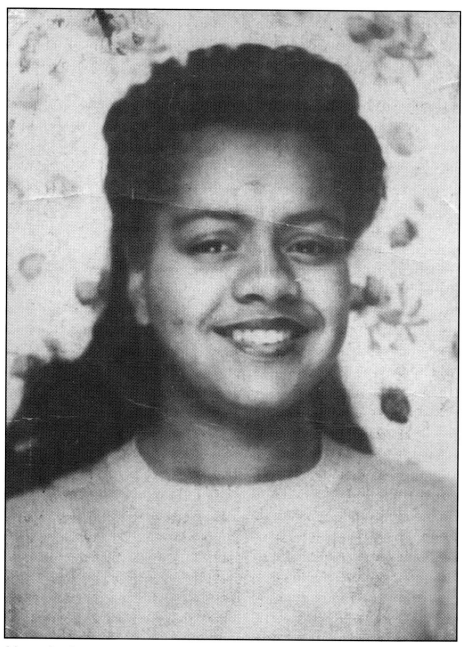

My mother Lucy, at age eighteen, smiling one of her few "true" smiles.

My mother at the
house on Tyler
Street resting after
a long day at work.

Three Arthurs—me,
my uncle Arthur
[center], and my father
[right]. Notice that
even here, the only
photo I have of him,
he's intoxicated.

Here I am [left] at about eight years old, with my brother Greg [top right], my sister Tracy [bottom right], and my cousin Kim [behind]. Notice I'm already preparing for a future in the military.

My cousins Rebecca, Kelly, and Kimberly, all of whom lived with us at the house on Tyler.

My sister Gale.

Me, in the United States Navy, 1975. If I had stayed there, I would have retired a year from now.

At Marquette Maximum Security Prison, 1983. Back then, we thought it was pretty cool to be "BAD!"

Jackson, 1988. I'm the fierce-looking one at the front of the rope with the hair-net. My team won the Firecracker-15 championship.

(Above) Me and Carl Merritt, Jr., the president of NAACP at Kinross Prison, at a Kawanza celebration. (Below) Jay Michaels and me working on the Coldwater prison newspaper.

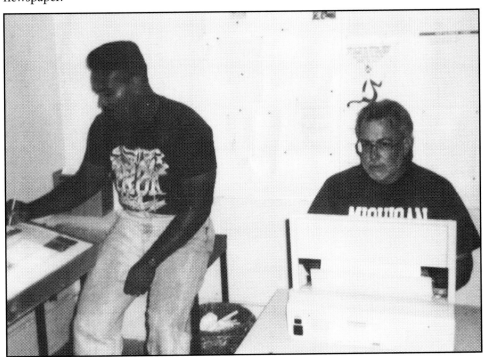

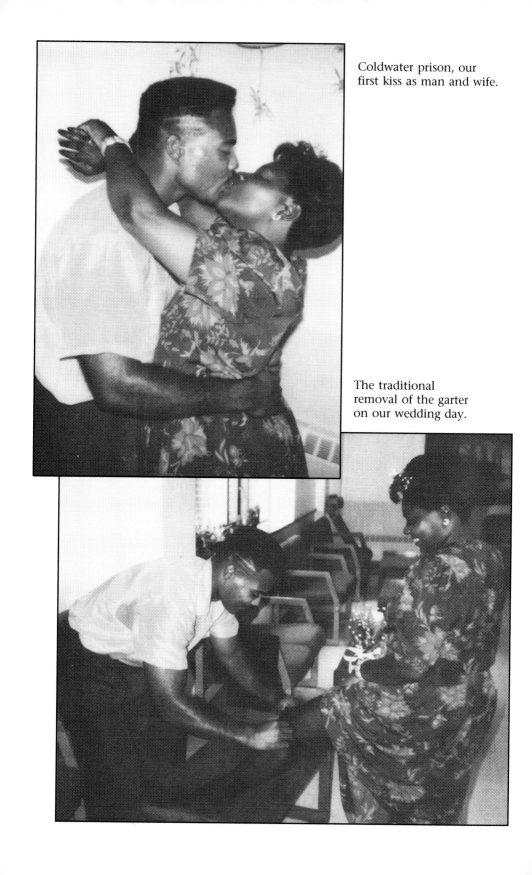

Coldwater prison, our
first kiss as man and wife.

The traditional
removal of the garter
on our wedding day.

My family at Christmastime, 1992.
My wife and I [above] at Kinross
Prison, and the kids at home [below].

Marilyn and me, dressed like twins, celebrating our first anniversary.

The family, before [above], and after, our marriage.

Marilyn and me on one of her frequent visits.

My son Omar, age 12. Since he's joined the family, his attitude and behavior has changed 180°, and his smile shows it.

My daughter Kyala is an outstanding student and wants to become a lawyer when she grows up and get me out of here.

My daughter Arlinda, has had the hardest time recovering from the environment she had with her mother; nevertheless, her progress has been slow but sure.

My daughter Chineca is the Tiger in the family and looks out for everybody. She is also an outstanding athlete and student.

My son Michael at
Niles High School
all decked out in
his football gear.
Michael has a 3.80
G.P.A., wants to
play college ball,
and then become
a doctor.

All the kids together in one portrait.

The president (me) and treasurer (Marilyn) of Fathers Behind Bars, Inc.

The newspaper staff at Kinross prison, many of whom were instrumental in helping give birth to the Fathers Behind Bars organization.

Teaching also reinforced my knowledge for my own intellectual purposes. Anyone who's taught will tell you that you always understand something better after you've had to explain it to someone else. Moreover, challenging questions from students can and do prompt the emergence of insights into things that otherwise might not be found.

For instance, once in a basic science class, some of the guys were not able to grasp the concept of humidity and why humid air impedes sweating and gives the feeling of mugginess. I wracked my brain to find a demonstration that would make the concept clearer than my verbal explanation or the textbook was able to do. This was not easy since there was no laboratory or scientific equipment available. They (the students) decided that since my proposition couldn't be demonstrated, it wasn't valid.

Just before the start of the class one morning, a solution hit me as I was washing my face. I came to class with what I hoped was make-shift but adequate equipment: two identical wash cloths, a tray of water and two empty calibrated beakers.

"Is that your scientific equipment, Teach?" the students teased me. "Yes..." I said confidently. I also reminded them that Newton had demonstrated gravity with an apple and Ben Franklin had demonstrated electric charge with a kite, a key, and a thunderstorm. This kept them quiet for a while. So I set about my work.

I dampened one washcloth with a certain amount of water measured from one of the calibrated beakers. I left the other cloth dry. The damp washcloth represented humid air and the dry one, of course, represented dry air. I dipped the damp washcloth into the tray of water then wrung the washcloth's water into one beaker; then I did the same with the dry cloth. Both beakers held about the same amount of water. But when we took the beaker that held water from the wet cloth and poured off the same amount of water we had originally dampened the wet cloth with, that beaker had less water than the one that held the water from the dry cloth.

This, I claimed, was analogous to the way that dry air holds more moisture and is therefore more conducive to evaporation and sweating. The wet cloth held less water and this inability to absorb moisture demonstrated humidity and the feeling of mugginess.

They got it. But in the tradition of skeptical jail-house lawyers, some of the students, who might be characterized as skeptical jail-house scientists, suggested that I might have rigged the experiment by wringing out the dry cloth harder, thus producing the added water I needed to prove my point.

One or two students were serious and even adamant. We repeated the experiment over and over. The skeptical students did it themselves wringing out the two cloths differently thus showing how I *could* have rigged the experiment. I did the experiment several times under their close scrutiny until most of the students were convinced. Finally, we voted to accept the results of the experiment as I had presented them and therefore the validity of the concept.

The students and I had had a tremendous intellectual work-out. We had also seen how concepts can be proven and not proven and how the truth can be manipulated.

Although the library was my original mental gymnasium, the classroom became my ultimate one. The exchanges that often went on there far exceeded what my solitary imagination could produce in the library. It was in the classroom, as nowhere else, that my mind grew in strength while that strength, in turn, benefited others.

Chapter 16

ANOTHER STORM

I had no idea what I was in for that day in October, 1982. I had been arrested yet another time. This time, my stay in the old (and I do mean *old*) Wayne County Jail would be longer than before.

It was like the dungeons you see in old horror movies. Dark and dreary, it had virtually no color and not much motion either. Things seemed to move in slow motion. It was as though the place I had entered was already in the past and it was still moving further back in time.

There was no spiraling network of cobwebs, like in those old movies, but I do think I might have seen a bat or two flying through the place and there were a lot of creepy, creaky cell doors.

I was twenty-four years old then. I had done time before and this place, though dismal and creepy, was not particularly foreboding. It was a close security jail and certainly not what was considered to be a place where somebody would do easy time.

One of the first things that the guy in the processing area asked me during my interview was whether I was "depressed." At first I thought it was some kind of trick, mind-game type of question. How could anybody not be depressed in a place like this? I remember thinking to myself as the interviewer waited patiently to scribble my answer. I knew what the truth was but I didn't know what the *right* answer was in terms of what was best for my future in that particular prison.

I looked at the interviewer closely. His face was like a bleak, almost blank sheet of white paper with vague, thin lines passing for facial features scratched across it. "Well?" He asked with a tone of irritation that had not been revealed in his face.

Eventually, i.e., in about fifteen seconds, I did as I suppose that mother would have wanted me to do; I threw caution to the wind and I told the truth.

"Yeah... I'm depressed." I said. I went on to speak in a way that would have really made my mother proud. I told the truth, the whole truth and nothing but the truth when I said: "Anybody would be depressed in a place like this, SHIT!"

I remember using that particular expletive very clearly, because later I was to think that I must have been clairvoyant.

The interviewer crumpled his face into a frown and concluded the interview with a few more questions.

Evidently I gave the wrong answer to either the "depression" question or one of the other things I was asked.

After the processing, I was taken from one of the dreariest areas I was ever in, to one of the smelliest.

I couldn't understand the odor. The place looked clean. The walls and floors seemed to have been washed or hosed down only a short time before I got there. The surfaces gleamed with moisture. But the odor persisted. Nothing was said to me.

A deputy sheriff brought me to my cell, unlocked it, put me inside, then swiftly locked the cell behind me and walked away with a disgusted look on his face. I settled down in the cell and started to put things in some kind of order; you know, clothes on shelves, Mom's picture on the desk, that kind of thing. Maybe I got used to the smell or something, I don't know, but I almost forgot about it. However, whenever I stopped and thought about it and took a deep breath, the smell was still right there. It was sickening. But I tried to keep my mind off of it by straightening up the cell.

Suddenly, a guy appeared at the cell door. He was white, he had long, matted hair and he had an expression on his face that was so tortured and crazed that it made Charles Manson's well-known visage look like that of an angel. The man was also completely naked.

"Hey..." He shouted at me from the other side of the bars of my cell door. "Have you seen that nigger, Peterson, this morning?"

"What?!?..." I replied in disbelief.

"I said 'have you seen that nigger, Peterson'... you heard me, nigger," the crazy-looking guy said.

Before I could answer an angry, black voice from outside of the cell answered for me:

"Hey, you white faggot... who you calling a nigger?!"

The white guy at my door turned in the direction of the voice. The moment he did, about a half-pound of human feces landed smack dab in his face.

He wiped the shit off his face as casually as a worker wipes off his sweat and said, "Oh, ya back, huh, nigger?... Stay right where you are and I'm gonna shove shit right down your throat and choke you to death!" With that, the guy at my cell door ran quickly back to his cell. I thought he was running to avoid being hit by more flying feces, but to my surprise, the guy reached into his toilet, grabbed a handful of his own excrement, and returned fire, so to speak.

These two equally mad (the black guy was naked and had hair matted with feces, too) men fought on and on. After ballistic attacks on each other, they engaged in hand to hand combat. They wrestled with each other on the floor, struggling and sometimes succeeding at stuffing feces into each other's eyes, nose, and mouth. It was disgusting.

Finally the deputy sheriffs came with hoses. They turned

the water on the two crazy guys full blast. Feces skeeted off of them in every direction. Some convicts cheered, others booed, and still others like me vomited. The stuff got into my cell and ruined a great many of my possessions.

Later, I found that I had been put on the psychiatric observation ward, largely because I had told that interviewer that I was depressed.

I begged them to believe that I wasn't depressed, and when the psychiatrist saw how happy I was when I was told I'd be removed from that floor, I'm sure he believed me.

Chapter 17

STEPPING OUT

The last time that I left prison was in 1981. I was determined never to come back. The guys in the prison were all very supportive. They told me that I was young and pretty smart, and that I had a real chance to make it.

I hoped that they knew what they were talking about. I figured that they did since they'd seen so many other guys come and go.

Then I remembered that I was no rookie myself. I had done time, and I had seen a thing or two. I started to think about what I had seen in all my years. I thought about the guys I'd seen come and go. The guys who had something on the ball and the ones who were just zeroes. Reluctantly, I began to believe what the guys who were trying to encourage me had said about making it this time in the free world and not coming back.

I was encouraged by the fact they hadn't talked to me like they did to a lot of guys who left who everyone *knew* were coming back. To those guys you'd hear things said like: "contact this guy for dope," or "make sure you call so and so for guns," or "stay away from that one... He's a terrible lawyer... He'll take your money, then sell you out."

That's not how they talked to me and I was encouraged by that. Instead they said things like: "Keep ya nose clean, kid," or "Fuck all the women for me in the free world." But the one I liked the most was from the guys who would be getting out later: "See you back in the free world, my brother." That's the one I savored the most. That's the one that meant at least two black men were going to be enjoying freedom.

But then I also began to figure how things work for most guys who get out and how they worked for me when I got out the last time. Who was I kidding anyway? Things didn't work out the last time. That's how I got back for my second stretch.

I got scared, really scared. But what could I do but just go out there and try?

I had re-established contact with my wife and we were going to try to make it again. What else was I going to try to do? I had to try.

I was truly frightened when I finally left that last day of my second sentence. I wondered about what courage meant and being brave meant. Did it mean not being afraid? If it did, then I had no courage. But if it just meant doing the right thing or just doing *some*thing in the face of impossible odds, well, maybe, just maybe, I could still make it this time. Maybe I had some courage and some worth after all. Maybe I could make myself worthy of respect. Shit, after thinking about it for a while, I didn't want courage, respect, awards, or any recognition for bravery—all I wanted was never to return to prison again.

Maybe I could become a real father, maybe find a job, maybe finish my education, and maybe even help other people. All those maybes. A torrent of them swept through my mind as I stepped out of prison that unusually warm day early in 1981.

But as the last gate of the prison closed behind me that day, one loud voice shouted in my mind's eye. It was as though a guy in the prison was yelling at me. Yelling to me from a window in the prison that he watched me from as I left. It was as though the guy had been reading my mind. The voice said: "Hey you!!!... yeah... you! Ya stupid fuckin' ex-con... I got a 'maybe' for you... *maybe* you'll be back!"

Chapter 18

MAXIMUM SECURITY

Remember how I said that it was an unusually warm day when I left prison in 1981? Well, things soon turned cold. Starting with my marriage and family. Nobody was really happy to see me. My wife was sort of surprised to see me. She actually had lost track of when I was getting out. Arlinda, my daughter, was barely three years old and knew nothing of me. She was still small, but was growing nicely. I desperately wanted her to know me better but the years that prison had taken from our relationship were gone forever.

I tried to reunite with my wife, but it was hopeless. The drift that had started before I went away continued and accelerated. We were going nowhere together fast. That kind of thing was all too prevalent in jail to have escaped the notice of a sensitive nose like mine.

Sweating during sex was another thing that I had not done for all the time I was in prison. After all if all you're going to do is choke your chicken, you won't be exerting yourself as much as you would when you got to handle a whole woman.

There were some exceptions to this in prison. I swear to God there were guys who would beat their meat so hard that you'd swear they were going to fracture their lower pelvis. These guys would make such a noise pounding their fists against their bodies, you'd think you were hearing a fight or something. Sometimes it was really grotesque.

It was great to be back with a woman. I loved it. Sometimes after intercourse, I'd just lay there in bed and take deep breaths. I'd savor the smell of my wife. She thought that I was some kind of freak for doing that, but that's just what I'd do. Sex was my only pleasure when I got out and I truly enjoyed it. But as for everything else, there was no pleasure or satisfaction of any kind.

First of all there was still no work, except for those jobs that just came and went. I really can't remember them that well. They all seem to just run together in my memory like some kind of dismal and miserable blur. Nothing lasted long, just enough for me to keep my head above water.

Later in '81, my son Omar was born. He was, of course, a not too surprising result of all the free-world sex I'd been having with his mother. But as I said before, he was, like his beloved sister before him, another reminder of my failure.

Maybe it was because he was my son. Maybe it was because he was born when I was out of prison and I was there to see it all. Or maybe it was for these reasons, added to all the hopes I had had when I left prison. But I hung in there and stayed away from crime... for as long as I could.

I took the bullshit jobs. The jobs that paid almost no money and never even allowed me to further my education. I often thought about that when I was busting suds in some greasy spoon or washing out a filthy toilet somewhere. I couldn't help but think that at least if I was in prison I'd be getting some kind of education. But I took all this for as long as I could. That was until 1982.

One night that year I just gave up, that's all. I gave up

hope for ever having more than the miserable little we had without picking up a gun again. We were living in a terrible place with broken doors and windows. The hallways were dirty. And the noise there was as loud sometimes as in prison. There were sirens, there was music, good and bad music, but both kinds were always too loud. There were people screaming at each other, screwing each other, beating each other, and sometimes even shooting each other.

What about welfare you might ask? Well welfare gave my family scarcely enough to cover the rent for where my family lived (officially I wasn't supposed to even be living there).

Their voices (those of my family's) were part of the chorus of pain and sorrow that was rising around me. In their various voices, they called out for more food, clean clothes, and a better place to live. The pitifully small amount of money that I was making was no answer to their cries.

And so once again I picked up a gun. Just as before, there were no bullets in the gun. And I hoped I'd be able to just take the money and run, and *nobody* would get hurt.

I went to where I knew there was always money, under the Golden Arches.

I walked into a McDonald's, introduced myself politely as a bandit who wanted to be taken seriously, and demanded money. I got it and before I left I couldn't help but say to the manager whose hands were high in the air: "This is for my kids."

He just sort of looked at me and said: "Okay sure uh-huh..."

I fled.

I hid out for a few days and then I returned to my home again. It was nowhere near Christmas but I was playing Santa Claus. Toys, gifts and most of all food, food that my son, who was not even a year old, had never eaten—food to make him grow. I also got them clothes and took them out a few places. I don't think I spent a dime on myself.

Then I did one of the strangest things I'd ever done in

my life. I went to my father's house. I don't know why, but I did. And for some reason I offered *him* some money. His second wife, Ida, suspecting the worst, told him to take nothing from me. But as he showed me to the door, he didn't resist taking it from me on the sly. He thanked me with a quizzical expression and asked me to never tell his wife.

I returned home and felt uneasy; I had a world-class case of a guilty conscious.

I had a guilty conscious and a sinking sense that I would not get away with what I had done. I guess the instincts of an old Navy man were working properly. I was picked up a few days after I had visited my father.

I was at my sister Tracy's house, they (the cops) just came by, found me there, and the next thing I knew, the handcuffs were going on and I was on my way out the door.

I had taken less than I did in my first robbery, only about two thousand dollars. I wasn't looking at an enormous amount of time, so therefore, what I did next seems even stranger, perhaps much stranger than my going to see my father, and a lot more stupid.

While being transferred from one holding area to another, I escaped. I just couldn't stand to go back to prison again. Just like I couldn't stand to have my kids go without food, I couldn't stand returning to prison.

While I was waiting uncuffed for one processing procedure or another, I just slipped out the door. It was the fall of 1982.

Was I chased? Well I suppose so, but not like they went after Richard Kimbal or anything. No hounds, no dragnets. Essentially, they did what they usually do with small-time crooks like me. They waited. They waited for me to screw up—like guys in my situation almost inevitably do—and that's what I did. I screwed up worse than I ever have in my life.

I went on the lam. I went to another town but I stayed in Michigan. I was at-large but I was no longer in what anybody would call the free world. I wasn't hunted but I knew I was being watched for.

I had no money. So I went back to the same bullshit

jobs that helped to drive me to commit the crime that had made me a fugitive. It's funny, but the best of these jobs is the one that led me back to prison.

It was November, 1982. I had gotten a good job as the assistant manager of a video arcade. It was the kind of job that if I had come across it months earlier, I never would have held up that McDonald's.

Anyway, things were going okay until one day, these guys came in and asked me to give a friend of theirs a job at the arcade. I didn't have the authority to hire anybody so I told them 'no.' They offered me money, much more money than the guy would have gotten paid if he had been hired.

By then it was clear; they were from a local gang and they wanted me to plant somebody there to sell drugs. *To sell drugs*!!!! They might as well have asked me to kill my own children. I had seen what drugs could do, what they had done to my brother. I practically threw them out of the place.

They came back a few days later, supposedly to just talk. When an arcade customer needed change, I went behind the counter to get it for him. That's when one of the guys from the gang confronted me, tried to intimidate me, and eventually pulled what I thought was a gun on me. I took the gun that the manager kept behind the counter and shot the guy first. I ran. The guy died shortly afterwards.

This time the police looked for me much harder. Just before Christmas 1982, they found me. I was taken in, convicted, and given a sentence of twenty-five to fifty years for armed robbery and twelve to fifteen years for manslaughter—an unheard-of sentence for the robbery I had committed. But it stuck and it sticks to me now.

Security is what I had always sought for myself and my family.

I felt a cruel sense of irony when the prison processing administration told me what my level of imprisonment was to be later that year when I started the term I'm serving now. "Mr. Hamilton," he said to me as my interview was completed. "You're on your way to Maximum Security."

Chapter 19

PRISON STORIES

These stories reflect one of the most important things that I was to learn in prison. Regrettably I had to learn this in the later part of my "career." If I had learned it earlier I might not be here today.

However, I did learn from these things, and fortunately, I didn't have to learn them the proverbial "hard way."

First, there was my good friend Rick, A.K.A. "Bullet." He was in for possession of heroin. That isn't why I became interested in him though. Like me, he was from a poor family, but in a rural part of the state. The lesson there being—poor is poor no matter how you slice it, and no matter where is occurs.

Rick's mother was on welfare, and, at the time I was speaking to Rick and learning about his life, his father was living and eating out of missions or shelters. Rick's life had been one mess after another. Like mine? Not really. You see, *both* of Rick's parents had taught and encouraged Rick and his siblings to steal.

He seemed surprised when I seemed surprised. Rick knew that what his parents had tried to instill in them was wrong and certainly not the norm (although I doubt Rick knew what a "norm" was). His parents had told their children that honest people were suckers and marks, and the only way to make it in the world was to take advantage of them, because that's what (now get this) "God had put them on the earth for!" Who the hell was their God—the devil? I wondered. But Rick was dead serious that this is what he'd been taught. And he learned nothing different from the criminal justice system he had come to be a part of. This is because he saw that the system was chock full of corruption in the police, the sell-out lawyers, the unsympathetic guards, the treacherous convicts, and even some money-grubbing foster-home parents, who only took in kids to get the money.

Rick told me honestly that it was guys like me, that talked about lives of hardship and love, brutality and Christian values, that made him really see that the world wasn't just made up of thieves and suckers. I had no idea that just telling my own story could ever have such an effect on another human being. Rick's revelation to me is one reason why I decided to write this book.

Next you should know about Tina. "Tina" is actually the prison name of a black, homosexual convict with whom I became friends. Tina became the source of many insights, not the least of which were the hypocrisy of some people who are supposed to be role models, and the suffering of gay people.

Years ago, Tina's father was a well-known and highly regarded preacher in Tina's hometown. But the good reverend was also a tremendous tightwad. Largely, because of their old man's cheapness, Tina and his kid brother stole a large amount of coal, with the idea of selling it to get spending money. Tina's father caught the then young boys hiding the stolen coal in the cellar of the church. The reverend brought down the wrath of God on the asses of his sons by beating them mercilessly. From Tina's description, the boys fared even worse than my family did at the hands of our father.

But the story does not end there. The reverend's church soon fell upon hard times. And Tina's father was forced to use the stolen coal to heat the church that winter. Quite by accident, Tina and Tina's brother discovered what was going on. The reverend swore both of them to "eternal secrecy."

Two Left Shoes

"Son, what you got dar?
I swear-for-God boy,
you always in trouble.
You go end up in jail yet."

"I's preach in church
fo' days a week, and
I's teaches what God says,
son."
"NO STEALING"
"NO LYING"
"NO CHEATING"
"NO KILLING"

"I's know we po', son.
And I's know black folk
tired uv having one prayer
a year answered.
Son yo' mama and I's ain't
got no money to get
yo'selfin out no slammer.
The po' peoples at church
a stealing mo' pennies from
the collection plate as
they's puttin' in.
Lemme see what you got
dar, son."

"Boy, I do declare, dis
here stuff you done gone
and stole is Black gold.
Dis here stuff is from
da earth's vault. You's
got a whole heap of dis
stuff boy. White folks and
Black folks—all folks, son,

needs dis here stuff when
da white rain lights the
night.
Run along now son, and don't
tells yo' momma nothing. She
worries herself in sick 'bout
everything, I do declare."

From this experience you would think that an eternal,
mutual bond was forged between the boys and the father,
not so. Tina said that when the reverend discovered that
Tina was gay, the right reverend completely and evidently
permanently ostracized Tina from the family.

Not My Choice

No place to go,
no blood of blood.
Expelled from the lives
of loved ones.
Cast out to lurk
among the shadows,
to shuffle among
my own; a hellish world.
Three tens
have passed me
by, five tens and
six I am.

Differences!!! Differences,
I say to you, have
damned me to hell.
No change! Never change!
I want to be
what I am.
Damn the preacher!
Damn the world!
My loneliness is
my haven; the shadows,
just intrusive silhouettes
of empty forms
void of compassion
and understanding.

My choice is my world.
I am what I am;
no change! Never change!
I can't go back to
what I never was. Damn the preacher!
Damn the world;
I am what I am.

This last story is simply one of addiction and cruelty. It was a story of crack and it's hold on a generation. Crack came into existence and prominence largely since I have been incarcerated. Even while I was out in the late '70s and early '80s I took little notice of the drug because I have never had any interest in hard-core drugs and because it was drugs that indirectly had cost my brother Greg his life. Add to this the fact that I had, at that time, seen virtually none of the ravages of crack on society first hand.

To illustrate for me the power of crack, a convict told me this story. He said that he was present once in a crack house when a fifteen-year-old girl, who was so strung out and in need of a hit of crack, told her fellow junkies that she would do *anything* for a "hit" of the drug. My friend explained that the girl had been a regular in the crack house for some time, and had already exchanged sex for crack with just about all of them, and so it was no longer considered by the male addicts as good enough of an exchange for the desperate girl to make.

And so the male addicts tried to come up with some task for the girl that would truly amuse them. All the while, the girl was going out of her mind with her desire for the crack. Finally, one of the addicts brought his vicious, snarling pit bull to the crack house. He told the desperate girl, that he would give her crack if she sucked the penis of the pit bull.

The male addict held the dog while the girl got down on her knees, fondled the dog, then started sucking the dog's penis. The other addicts roared with laughter. Finally, after some minutes, the girl looked up from what she was doing and asked for her crack. "Keep sucking!" The men replied.

Finally, when the sight of what the girl was doing was no longer funny, the man who held the dog released it and the dog snapped it's powerful jaws at the girl's bobbing head. "Keep sucking, bitch!!!" The men demanded and that's exactly what the girl did. For how long? The guy who told the story had no idea as he left after about an hour.

These stories, and many others I would hear, let me know that my life, though bitter and hard, was not the worst any man had ever lived that landed in prison. And for that I give thanks to this day.

The worst I had seen and experienced was simply that. It was not nearly the worst of all. The pain, anguish, and desperation contained in these stories explained the pain, anguish, and desperation that I saw, but did not experience myself (at least to the extremes I saw it experienced) in prison life.

Children Reflected

In this world of ours,
where so many things are wrong;
where mothers abandon their babies,
and fathers refuse to be strong.

Where illiteracy runs rampant,
and politicians lie;
where media deceives the public,
while homeless people die.

In this world of ours,
where much evil abounds;
demonic forces everywhere,
in many hearts it pounds.

In this world of ours,
the people must take a stand.
We must protect the flowers,
we must protect the land.

We must protect the children,
cling tight with all our might.
They will one day be our future,
so teach them wrong and right.

Chapter 20

THE TIME MACHINE

The start of my current sentence seemed like the beginning of the end, not the *rest,* of my life.

Prison society is like a society of scared, untamed, parentless, and homeless children. The kind portrayed in the book, *Lord of the Flies.* There is no society at all in here. There are just kids of all ages trying to deal with their homelessness and lack of positive guiding forces or role models by setting up mock governments and making rules the way they think grown-up or free world people do.

Prison is the desert island that most will never escape from.

I think that groups, whether they are great civilizations or a few hundred prisoners, are prone to make the same great mistake. The mistake is they think that all you need to make things work is: a sense of common identity, work, law, order, and maybe religion. This is inadequate and you can see that in prison. You need family structure of some type or another to make a prison society work.

But then there really is no such thing as prison *society*. All that is supposed to exist in prison is, a group of men living (for lack of a better term) in the same place. This is not civilization, society, or family. This is a gang or mob existence. Prison may not be cruel and unusual punishment, but it is also not effective socialization. Restraint can be learned in here but not human values. Human values can't be taught without families.

In the days before television, prison must have been profound isolation. The convict got out of jail and found a whole new world on the outside. Everything was new and unfamiliar—clothes, cars, machines, buildings—everything. It was as if the convict had been placed in a time capsule, and exhumed at the end of his sentence.

That's not the way it is in the television age; Now prison is more like a time machine rather than a time capsule. Just like in the famous H.G. Wells' story, inmates *see* the world through the window of television as it changes, as it is passes them by...

All through the '80s I could see America getting more violent, less caring, and more greedy. I could see it on television. And thanks to reruns, I could see and compare how things, values in particular, had changed in relation to years gone by.

In the '60s, shows about traditional families abounded. But in the '80s, with the exception of "Cosby" and a few others, true-to-life cop shows and syndicated tabloid news programs were the coming thing.

We went from a time when the nation was held spellbound by the plight of the falsely accused man, i.e., "The Fugitive", to the true-to-life cop shows that are nothing more but video tape of cops chasing people who have not been convicted of anything.

Even the popularity of "Cosby" during the '80s was deceptive. The show wasn't popular because the family life portrayed was typical. Instead I think that "The Cosby Show" was popular because in part, families such as the show depicted were disappearing in the free world. All my reading, and my reading was and is extensive, told me that across the board in America, families were getting smaller, less affluent, and less stable.

Free world America was getting very mean and so were the men coming into prison. Guys from broken homes have always found their way to prison but the guys I saw coming through in the '80s were a different breed.

They were getting meaner, the younger guys who were coming in during that period. More of them came not just from second and third generation welfare homes, but from second, third, and fourth generation criminal homes—i.e., homes where parents, grandparents, and even great grandparents had been incarcerated for serious crimes.

How could this be? Simple. The "generations" were shrinking; kids were having kids or rather, babies were having babies in a way that I had never seen before.

Also, more and more guys were coming in who had no families at all, other than perhaps from scattered foster home placements.

What worried me most was that *my* kids were becoming part of the same trend. I was in prison; they were in what could be described as nothing better than an unstable situation, and they were on welfare.

My sisters were telling me bad things about how my kids were being taken care of. The worst part of it was the example that their mother, my wife, was setting for them. It was bad enough that my kids had a father in prison, that was my fault. They didn't have to ever be told who or where I was. The less they heard about a father in prison, the better, if that would help matters. But they had a mother who was using drugs and that was something that they were seeing every day of their young lives.

I had just about come to the point of accepting the fact that I would probably not see the other side of prison walls for the balance of the twentieth century.

But the possibility that one of my own children could join me in prison was too much to stand.

Chapter 21

MARILYN

Remember the dreams I described in the first chapter? The part of those dreams that haunted me the most was seeing the faces of my children appear at my cell door and then slowly deteriorate into two of the countless skulls.

To me, the skulls represent wasted lives. Lives that my incarceration has helped to destroy because I have failed someone as a son, as a brother, as a friend, or even just as a black man who wasn't there when someone needed me.

One face that never appeared in my dreams to haunt me was my present wife, Marilyn. She has been my savior. Without her I would have long since turned into one of the sad and terrible creatures that I have described in this book.

Marilyn's love is the only reason why I am still in this world, and her strength is what will keep me here while I serve the rest of my sentence. You see it is Marilyn, more than anyone else, who has made it even possible for me to call myself a Father Behind Bars.

I met Marilyn through her brother, George. I met him

almost by chance. He landed in my prison in 1987, and of course, the story how he had gotten there was making the rounds.

It seems that he was in for a conviction of robbery. This was not unusual. Neither was the fact that he said he was innocent—hell, I was innocent too! I said to myself as I reluctantly accepted George's court papers from him to read one day in early 1987.

I had become somewhat of a jailhouse lawyer/ counselor/guru. Well, actually any guy who had a long sentence, had served a significant portion of it, and still had his wits about him was well-regarded and therefore, often sought after for advice.

As I thumbed through George's papers, I could see that he had indeed been railroaded. He had been instructed to plead guilty to everything that he had been charged with. He was not even aware of some of the things he had been convicted of. He claimed that his lawyer had never interviewed him other than to drill him on the instructions for his pleading.

The pre-sentencing report clearly indicated that George had a tenuous connection to the cases that he was supposed to be involved in. Yet, he was severely sentenced anyway.

But what incensed me most of all was the fact that George was a sick man. He was taking medication for schizophrenia. He was barely functional. I was also mad because George had a family, and I couldn't see where the family had been helping him.

A man with a family had an advantage—I thought— and I wanted to know why George had been denied this advantage. I assumed that George had been abandoned by his family the way I had been by mine. But I was wrong.

Without George knowing, I called his home to get some answers. I got the answers I was looking for and more. The person that I spoke to on the phone listened carefully, then she let me have it. That person was Marilyn. The woman who would become my wife.

Marilyn told me in great detail how difficult her struggle had been. She told me that much of what I had told her about her brother's case she had never heard. She had not heard it from either her brother or from his lawyer. The lawyer part of this communication breakdown made sense, since this was the same lawyer that had misled her brother. As to why her brother had never shared the full picture with her, we concluded that he had given up on himself at about the same time his lawyer had betrayed him. His lawyer had never told him that his condition was a basis for different treatment before the law and so he had accepted all that came his way.

But during our discussions about her brother, I came to know Marilyn's story. How she was trying to raise her three children with no help from anyone. She and her family had come to this country from their native Jamaica in the West Indies, in 1967. She was nine years old.

Her siblings, who are younger than she, had all, with the exception of her brother, gone on to educate themselves and had gained good professional positions. After graduating from high school, Marilyn chose to work and try to start a family with the father of her children. Marilyn had her first child when she was in high school, but she still graduated on time.

Marilyn was indeed a very strong woman and she had come from a strong family. It was a close knit and very industrious family with strong sense of values. But when they came to America, her family entered the black community and found no fulfillment and no understanding. The chief problem was the difference in values. Her family found that poor American blacks were willing citizens in the American welfare state, which was something that was virtually unknown in Jamaica. In Jamaica there was a strong work ethic even for the poor people. People with nothing often worked for little more than nothing. But here the story was different and very unfamiliar to Marilyn and her family. To them work was not *a* way of life, it was *the* way of life.

Marilyn's mother was a village family photographer. And her father was an agricultural laborer. Her father, who has always been a tremendous inspiration to Marilyn, lost his left hand when he was about eighteen. He lost it loading sugar cane into a cutting machine. He almost bled to death. But his fellow workers donated their blood to him and his life was saved. Marilyn likes to say that good things can come from bad and vice versa. The blood that the workers donated to her father saved his life, but doctors also believe that that blood might have been responsible for the sickle-cell trait that Marilyn and her siblings have in their blood today. In any event, Marilyn's father went back to work in less than two weeks and he never missed another day of work during the rest of his working life. He retired in 1991 at the age of sixty-five.

Moreover, poor black Americans seemed to have been beaten down and plagued with low self-esteem. Marilyn often found personal character in individual black Americans to be as weak as the family structures they were part of and the work ethic they held. They were glad, or at least willing, to take welfare. Marilyn's family found the welfare system degrading, not the state of poverty itself.

In addition to this, Marilyn clearly found problems with American black men. Dope was a big problem. Her spouse, just like mine, had fallen victim to this scourge. In the years that followed the time that Marilyn and her siblings came to this country, drug abuse would invade their native land. And it would prove to be as devastating there as it had already become here. But when they left Jamaica, aside from marijuana use, there was virtually no problem. Therefore, nothing prepared her for what she was to find here.

She was also not prepared for the sort of black male that she found here in America. In Jamaica, black males are feisty, macho, vigorous, and passionate towards their women. Here in America, Marilyn found many black males less willing to lead in relationships. She also found them laid back, indifferent, if not totally uncaring, even while in relationships with her.

In the course of our getting to know each other we discovered many things. And discovery, particularly self-discovery, is an essential part of any relationship. Marilyn and her values taught me that I was not a fool or a misfit for wanting a lasting, balanced, and fully shared relationship. I taught her that black American men with strong family values did exist—at least that's what I'm still trying to prove both to her, my children, and to myself.

Love did not come easily or immediately to Marilyn and I. As I told you, Marilyn is a hard realist. And she could see that there was little future in a relationship with a guy who might not see freedom until sometime in the next century.

And so we stuck to other issues, how to get useful answers to pressing problems. We had some victories. Working together we set Marilyn's brother on a course to full recovery and rehabilitation. He is now out of prison, working and living independently. The road has not always been smooth for him on the outside. And when he has faltered, Marilyn has sent him to see me here in prison, where both listening to me and seeing these gray walls once more has always put him back on the right track.

Marilyn gave me the courage to fight for my children. She kept my mind focused on them at points of despair when my own strength was gone.

It was Marilyn that was my emissary to my sisters. She went to them and started the healing process that resulted in their being reunited with me.

Marilyn also paid me the high honor of bringing *her* children into my life. You can't imagine how touched I was the first time she brought them to meet me. Her children were all immaculately dressed. They were all impeccably groomed and similarly well-mannered. And when they spoke, they spoke graciously, intelligently and sincerely. Most touching was what they spoke about. They talked about me and my life as well as theirs. Marilyn had already told them about me; I had existed in their lives before she brought them to meet me.

Marilyn introduced me to them as the man who had helped their uncle and who helped her to know the ways of this country better. I felt so proud that for the first time, and for a while, I forgot that I was in prison.

But as I said, Marilyn is smart and realistic, as well as being thankful and kind. She also wanted her children to see that even people with good hearts and minds can end up in prison. She made it clear to me that she wanted her children to know that mistakes can put you in prison. And after you're in, the best of intentions cannot release you. Even though I was in part an object lesson in how *not* to ruin your life, I still felt honored and deeply moved.

Marilyn told me that my explanation of the way black American males act toward women helped her self-esteem. It wasn't hard for me to be honest about that. I knew how disrespectful black American men could be; I had been one of those types myself. But I feel that she did much more for my self-esteem than I did for hers. In total, I feel she has done a lot more for my life than I have been able to do so far for hers.

Other than my own mother, I have never met anyone so completely committed to her family and work. Her stories of her native Jamaica were always filled with accounts of family and their work. Her family worked in farms, factories, market places, hotels, anywhere the work was hard and steady paying. She told me that she and her siblings had been raised to avoid easy jobs because easy jobs were a sign of bad business management, and businesses that are not well run, will not last.

As for her family, even though they were separated by the distance from America to Jamaica they were still as one. Money, letters, gifts, phone calls, and encouragement flowed steadily back and forth between family members in both countries. Nothing could separate them. They had their share of disputes but nothing destroyed the fiber of their family ties.

As fortunate as she was, in having a strong, supportive, unbroken family, Marilyn also made her own luck and she earned every one of her blessings through hard work. This I admired and respected most of all. Today, Marilyn works as both a painter on an automotive assembly line and a part-time cook.

As I said earlier, love came slowly, but admiration and respect came quickly and has never waned. When she brought her kids to see me, I knew that we were building something, but I wasn't sure what it was. We all just kind of blended together into a loving unit. The only thing that was missing was my own children.

The sincere way her children responded to me gave me courage and hope. It gave me hope that I could still be regarded as, and actually feel like, a man and a father. In addition, Marilyn put me to work as a father. She had me tutor and counsel her children. She brought their homework, their report cards, their accomplishments, and their problems right to me there in the prison. And when that wasn't possible, we were on the phone talking things out. Struggling, loving, failing, and succeeding just like a free-world family. A family without my kids and with a father in prison, but a family just the same.

All this is what our later love was based on and Marilyn and I were getting closer as a couple all the time.

But the impossibility of a real romance haunted the relationship. How or why would anyone seriously consider falling in love with a man who might not be free for another ten or fifteen years? That's what we kept telling ourselves, but that's not what was in our hearts. And that's not what we were seeing in each other's eyes.

Finally, recognizing that we were falling in love, we did as we had done on other issues. We confronted our attraction to each other head-on, and we grappled with it thoroughly.

We went to what we thought was the central point: How could we express affection for each other if I was locked up? We knew all the positives: We liked each other, loved each other, loved and respected the kids— and they us, and my existence and my spiritual presence in their home was good for everybody. But the negative of not being able to consummate things still loomed large. We were just about to set the issue aside and declare ourselves totally and officially in love when we realized something and asked ourselves another question: How will we all feel about each other when the day of my freedom arrives, and how will we make out in the years that will follow? We both knew of so many cases where romances like ours, that started in prison, had soured when the inmate was released.

We had given ourselves an absolute deadline to either go forward as life partners for the duration or to continue as close friends until I was released and see what happened as we went along. When the day for the decision came, we put everything on the table and tried to talk each other, and ourselves, out of having a romantic relationship. But it didn't work, we were hopelessly in love. We kissed each other passionately that day in the visiting room. Even with everyone watching—including our kids—we kissed with reckless abandon. We attracted a lot of attention. Kissing was allowed during visits, but only at the start and at the end of the visit and only briefly at any time.

Just before a guard who had been watching came over, we stopped. We decided to go over and announce our commitment to the children. When we did they almost laughed in our faces. They knew and had known for some time that we were in love. To just about everybody else but us it was only a matter of time before we announced what was never really a secret.

But we did have one surprise for everyone. We told them that we would soon be married.

Chapter 22

WORDS: MY WINGS OVER THESE WALLS

I soon found that getting married to Marilyn was much harder than I expected. To begin with, I was still married to my first wife. This meant having to get a divorce from her.

I had no money for a lawyer, so I decided to at least try to do as much of the work as possible. I got all the papers together and began to put the case together. Although the task was not an exceedingly hard one, it did challenge my knowledge and ability. I was forced to work that much harder and improve my skills. This meant constant study of grammar, vocabulary, sentence structure, and parts of speech. I wanted to be able to do more than just write letters and ask for somebody to help me. I wanted to be able to understand every step of a proceeding and present detailed arguments of my own.

And with the constant encouragement of Marilyn, I began to even look past the goal of winning a divorce, further into the future to the point of being able to go into court and win custody of my children. Some dream, I thought to myself.

Once again I was back in the gymnasium of the mind, the library. I studied and wrote and studied and wrote. All this preparation drew attention. The word about what I was doing got around. Anytime *anybody* does anything to a furious extent in prison, the word gets around. Guys asked me to write things for them, letters mostly, but also statements and wills. I never charged a fee though. Writing was my gift from God. Therefore, I thought that I was supposed to share it at no charge to my fellow man. Marilyn didn't always agree with this. But as long as I kept my eyes on the prize, which was to do my own work, we remained in agreement.

Soon the opportunity to write for another prison newspaper came, and I jumped at it. The newspaper meant access to a better typewriter just about all the time, as well as more reference books and a community of other writers too. I would later become editor of that paper.

My preparation for the divorce was going ahead smoothly. I had gone over the papers, checking them for errors and completeness. I knew that I had done everything that I could on this score and so I just waited for the date when I was to hear from the court.

On the day before the decision about the divorce was to come, I was sitting in my cell, and a guy came by and said he had read a particular article I had written. He said something that I have never forgotten: "Man..." he said. "Your words are powerful, someday you're going to write your way out of here."

Those words have always stuck with me. Even when the denial of my divorce came back from the court, those words stuck with me. I kept writing. And I never stopped.

Marilyn was the first person to tell me not to be discouraged. If she had not done so, then I don't know what I would have done. I wanted to do something to show her just what she had meant to me. Something that only I could do. I started writing her poetry. It was supposed to be just for her, but ultimately one of the guys who was always coming around hunting for some of my work to read found one or two of the poems and read them.

Word got around about the poetry, too, and I was asked to write something for an upcoming event. Not wanting to share my love poems with the whole world, I wrote about the environment I had come from, a life that still surrounded me. The name of the poem was "RAT RACE."

I wrote it, submitted it, then forgot about it. I went back to trying to deal with my own problems, i.e. everyday prison survival. It was about that time that I witnessed a knife being plunged into an inmate's heart by another prisoner. Few things can take your mind off of esthetic contemplation quicker than seeing someone put to death.

All was not a bed of roses in the newsroom either. For one thing, someone, to this day I can't determine who, wanted my job as editor of the prison newspaper. They evidently wanted it so badly that they planted a knife in my office. I was put in isolation for the full week until my case came up. I sat in isolation dreaming that terrible dream of suicide and saying to myself, why *not* do it? Why not just kill yourself and be done with? You're never getting out of prison, and you'll never be with Marilyn and your children as a free man anyway.

When they finally let me out, I knew in an instant that I had done the right thing in trying to hold on. Marilyn visited me the next day as proof positive of that choice. At the hearing, I was found not guilty. I was surprised that both the Warden and Deputy Warden spoke up for me, but that's what they did.

This would not be the last time that I would lose my job as editor though. Once, I wrote a story that criticized Michigan Governor James Blanchard for his prison policies. The year was 1990. Even though it was never published in a prison newspaper, word of it's basic arguments and my censorship spread quickly. It shook the entire prison system and I stood alone. I was asked to resign and I did. I sent the story to Grand Rapids Press and *they* ran it. It also found its way to the AP. Some days later, I was hired as a teacher's aide.

Anyway, I was so genuinely happy to be out of isolation, back with Marilyn, and back at the paper that I forgot about the poem RAT RACE completely. You can therefore imagine how shocked I was when I found out that it had won a free-world poetry competition. I was asked to read RAT RACE at a special ceremony.

When the day arrived, I was terribly nervous. Anxiety was temporarily replaced by pride and joy until I learned who else was in the audience. Among the many dignitaries that were there was Ms. Gail King, a prominent educator and the niece of Malcolm X. Once again I was a bundle of nerves. As I waited to read my poetry, I glanced out in the audience and saw two empty seats together near the front row. For some reason, I thought about my mother and my brother and I wondered, no hoped, that their spirits were there.

The time came for me to read and so I did. The audience really seemed to love what I had written. Convicts and the black prison guards were on their feet barely a moment before the rest of the audience. Everyone was cheering. That wonderful moment is one of the reasons that I continue to write poetry.

Ms. King gave me a truly wonderful congratulation. She said that she was both moved and inspired by my poetry. To have the flesh and blood of one of my greatest heroes compliment my work was a great thrill.

As I turned to leave the stage, I looked back to see those two seats, still empty, still symbolizing the spirits of my mother and brother. They were telling me that I was doing the right thing, that I was headed the right way. At the very least I felt that words would be part of the rest of my life, and that perhaps words might someday become my wings over the walls of the prison.

Rat Race

Rat Race, rat race, Come one, come all,
see the man in the ghetto who feels two feet tall.
Rat race, rat race, come one, come all,
Watch the po' man take a po' man's fall.

See the ghetto's circus, its clowns and fools,
observe the Black man's houses, his towns and schools.
Rat Race, rat race, come one, come all,
when a Black man is dying, who's he gonna call?

Come to the ghetto and see the lions and bears,
new-wave crime, and brand new dares.
Come one come all, cause we won't hide,
when unemployment went up, we lost our pride.

Lil' Black kids, dirty and crying,
young black men in the streets dying.
America! America! You claim to be a "Great Nation,"
but degradation, suffocation, and humiliation is your creation.

I speak the truth, 'cause I've seen from day one,
that when the truth is presented, you grab your gun.
You speak of PEACE and DEMOCRACY,
Well, I call it an atrocious HYPOCRISY.

Where did it start? And where will it end?
Is the answer just around the bend?
It started with the ghettos and there it will stop,
'cause America's system is a piteous flop.

Rat Race, rat race, don't pass me by,
allow me to keep pace and don't ask me "Why?"
So come one, come all, from east, west, north, and south.
Hear our babies cry when they open their mouths.

Come to the circus and see the monkeys with guns,
observe only, because interference would be no fun.
See the lions bully the weak, and the tigers rob the dead,
then try to figure this shit out in your Harvard trained heads.

Infest the circus with rats, roaches, and mice,
then expect poor people to be patient and nice.
It's a hell of a world, a hell of a place,
To sum it all up; it's a fucken rat race.

Who am I to sum this up?
I'll tell you.

I'm not a pimp or a player, I'm considered a prince,
I don't use slick lines, I just use common sense.
I was named "Arthur" just like the king,
songs of despair and poverty is what I sing.

Lock me up throw away the key, put me on a prison diet,
but none of this bullshit will keep me quiet.
I'm a child of the lost, perhaps an angel in disguise,
because all the aforementioned shit, has made me wise.

Laugh at me, ridicule me, but don't spit in my face,
Because then, I, Arthur, will put you in your place.
And if you're looking for the end, this is only the beginning,
now that I have your attention, I feel I'm winning.

So you've heard my grievances and my complaints,
on the rulers of this nation, we use restraints.
The rulers of this nation are the true crooks,
disguised in their glasses and Clark Kent looks.

They've robbed the Black man blind for so many years,
created chaos among Black people with stupid ass fears.
The characteristics of the Black man are divided by three.
The "I don't give a fuck," the House Nigger, and the crazy.

Dope in our neighborhoods—what a mean, but intelligent plan,
yet when it reached the White neighborhoods, it was wrong,
    understand?

The shit they're throwing at us, let's return the favor,
but we will add spices, that will make a nice flavor.
PRISONS and FRONTLINE WARS are their specialities,
poor po' man, facing these horrified realities.

But there's a catch in the scheme, and it's called catch
    twenty-two,
having to be content with this shit is very untrue.
Po' man just step back and fold your arms,
let the rich fight the wars while we tend the farms.

Catch twenty-two had been around forever,
to understand its value, one must truly be clever.
The rich define it as having twenty-two catches and a
    Remington trigger,
learned how to use it against the much oppressed nigger.

The solution to the problem is very simple,
you just squeeze the rich like you squeeze your pimple.
Rat race, rat race, what a crying shame,
rich taking advantage of the poor and the lame.

Remember I said, "The characteristics of the Black man are
    divided by three?"
Well let me explain, so listen *CLOSELY!*
Rat Race, rat race, "Please stay out of my way."
This is what the "I don't give a fuck nigger" has to say.

He's content in the suburbs, with his trimmed green grass,
abandoned the less fortunate, frighteningly fast.
Climbs the ladder by using his Black brother's head,
our children are skinny, while his kids are well fed.

Turn their heads on our problems as they become worse,
scared we might hold out our hands, so they hide our purse.
Rat race, rat race, this is what I figure,
now let me explain the house nigger.

He's a cobra, a rattler, a boa constrictor all in one,
"Yes em boss, de nigga actin up, let me git de gun."
"Alright nigga, fall yo' ass in line,
fo' massa have me put a whip to yo' Black behind."

He's the type of person who would be your friend one day,
but when the White man is around, he's your adversary,
in an inexplicable ass way.
He's got poison in his mind, and venom in his bite,
and he will buckle under pressure when the White man
   makes it tight.

That's when his snakish ways against his people comes in,
a low blow and K.O. to the vulnerable chin.
Take my advice concerning this man,
stay away at all costs if you possibly can.

Rat Race, rat race, this is the last of the three,
this is the most important; alleged to be *"Crazy."
The crazy man is the Black man's salvation and only hope,
he can draw more attention than the Catholic Pope.

He will confront wrong, for every right reason,
ain't scared of committing high treason.
This is the hardcore who've seen it all,
witnessed landlords steal us blind, and families fall.

Watched Mama scrub floor, clean White men's stools,
experienced White men's schemes that left them feeling
   like fools.
In the 1960's, got radical and glued fingers to triggers,
then was sold out by the snakish house niggers.

This left them feeling lonely, defeated, and confused,
a different story for many Whites, they were chillingly amused.
The hardcore minority, is in a class of his own,
he won't bow for Whites, this he has shown.
*Crazy as in Malcolm X, King, Bico... Southern Whites
    referred to
men who fought tooth and nail against racism as
    "Crazy niggers."

Although he is direct, he is also clever,
knowing when to stand alone, and when to stand together.
Government spends thousands just to figure out his mind,
but he shuts them out and no weakness shall they find.

So when it's time to confront, just call on this unique man,
because direct confrontations is what oppression understands.
Some think it's impossible to unite the three,
but until this occurs, we will not be free!

Rat Race, rat race, what a hell of a man,
seems that he's the only one to understand:
That the poor has risen to many; the rich to fewer,
and his childrens' dreams are fading down a stinkin' sewer.

Chapter 23

ONE FAMILY

I continued my struggle on all fronts. I kept writing and teaching convicts. I kept studying both in class and on my own. I kept on writing letters and drafting memoranda for an appeal to reduce my sentence. I kept preparing and checking the papers for another attempt at being granted a divorce from my first wife. And I kept writing to social workers and the department of Children's Protective Services to be granted custody of my children. I had to let my job as teacher's aide go. It was just too much. Something had to give and I guess it had to be that. I still tutored informally because I missed teaching and the guys really needed it. But the teaching load I had been carrying was gone.

In terms of my own education things seemed to be going well. I had earned my GED and kept on going with college classes. Slowly but surely the credits just kept piling up on my transcript—an associates degree was clearly within my grasp.

Then for the first time in my life I became a prisoner of positive choices. My prison record had been good in terms of my behavior. In fact, at the juncture in question, it was excellent. I was therefore given the opportunity to be transferred to a safer, lower security prison. At such an institution, virtually everything would be better. There would be better facilities, more visiting time with Marilyn and her kids, and a better, less violent, class of inmates to be living with. There was, however, one drawback—the lower security institution might not have college courses. So there it was. Either I stayed where I was and finish my college studies in that hellish environment I was in, or I took a chance, went elsewhere, and possibly ruin my chances for earning a degree.

As always, I talked it over with Marilyn. We decided that I would stick it out where I was. During the rest of the time that I was there, I saw many gruesome things, including one of my colleagues at the paper get his throat cut from ear to ear. He survived but only because of the grace of God and good, prompt medical care.

One year after I decided to remain at Northside Jackson prison, I picked up my Associates Degree diploma from Jackson Community College. The year was 1988. I graduated among the top fifty students in the entire college—that included free-world graduates. I had a 3.68 average. Once again, miraculously, there were two empty seats in a row near the front of the auditorium just as there had been when I read my poem. And just as before, I felt the spirit of my mother and of Greg.

During this time, I also won an award for prison journalism from the School of Journalism at the Southern Illinois University in Carbondale, Illinois. The award was for : "The best prison paper in the entire country..." and I had been the editor.

As I said, I continued the letter-writing campaigns for my court cases. I got back courteous responses but no commitments or encouragement, which was about what I had expected.

Nothing seemed to be changing right up to that day in 1990, when a guard woke me up and told me to hurry and get out of my bunk, because I had a court appearance that morning. I didn't remember any court date, but I figured it was concerning one of the many letters I had written about my appeal to have my sentence reduced. They rushed me so much that I didn't have time to bathe, brush my teeth, or call Marilyn. I was out of there before I knew what was happening.

I had just about decided to "go with the flow" as the van that was transporting me pulled away from the prison. But then I noticed that the van was not heading to the court that was supposed to be hearing my appeal, so I asked where I was being taken. The reply I got from the guard and the driver was that I was indeed headed to court, so again I became silent.

Finally we pulled up to the Probate Court, which is where juveniles appear for court procedures. Then and only then did I realize that this trip to "court" was about my children. My mind began racing over terrible possibilities: Were the kids sick or something... Had there been an accident... Had their mother finally OD'd? What was going on? Of course, neither the guard nor the driver knew anything except when and where I was to go. So I remained silent but I wanted to scream.

I also considered the terrible way I looked. I was unwashed and chained torso, hands and legs. This was not the way I wanted my children to ever see me. *Being* in prison is something that they were used to, but they had never seen me looking like a bum nor had they ever seen me in chains.

Those particular fears were soon proven unjustified. There was no one in the courtroom where I was taken to but a judge, who was an African-American woman, an attorney, some court personnel, a couple of social workers, and myself. I had been brought there to be apprised of what was going on in the home where my kids were living.

The attorney explained to me that my kids were in trouble. Arlinda, my daughter, had already been committed to the state and my son, Omar, was having severe problems in school and at home. Lastly, I was informed that Linda, their mother and my wife, was facing charges of neglect. When I heard this it seemed as a great weight had fallen right on me that instant. I almost slumped to my knees right then and there in the court as I felt tears coming into my eyes. The judge said that there was a possibility that the kids might have to be placed in one or more foster homes.

"Noooo!" I shouted there in court with my fists clinched and quivering and my chains rattling. "Please don't do this, your honor." I pleaded.

The judge looked sympathetic but she asked me for an alternative.

I immediately asked that each of my children be placed with my sisters until Marilyn and I were married, at which time I assured the judge that they (my children) would then be sent to live with Marilyn and her children. A social worker who was present spoke up and agreed with my suggestion, saying that she knew of the fitness and character of everyone I had just mentioned as potential guardians, because I had made this proposal in writing some time before. The social worker held up many of my letters that I had written to her as she spoke.

The judge asked to see my letters. The social worker handed them over and stepped back from the bench while the judge read. The judge read at least two letters carefully. Then she perused the rest. Then the judge announced her decision.

The judge went from being sympathetic to being persuaded. Linda had failed to appear at this hearing and at an earlier one. Based on this, and what she had just heard, the judge awarded custody of my children to my sisters pending my marriage to Marilyn. My sister Gail was to take Arlinda and my sister Tracy took Omar.

Now the tears really flowed, but they were tears of joy and relief.

Everyone in the court room seemed happy for me. I must have looked so pitiful standing there unwashed, in chains and in tears, even if they were tears of joy.

Everyone in my family was happy too. We were all happy. But we knew that much working and waiting still remained before us. We set about putting the two families together immediately. We made my children, Arlinda and Omar, part of Marilyn's spiritual household right away.

My sisters were exceedingly supportive. They understood and performed their roles as temporary guardians to absolute perfection. Although my mother would have never imagined the exact circumstances, it was just the way she had always hoped and, of course, prayed, her children would blend together—in loving cooperation as adults.

Two more years passed, bringing more disappointments in court with respect to both my divorce from my first wife and my appeal. In one sense, it didn't matter. We became one family spiritually soon after the judge's decree that kept my children out of foster homes. It has been the seven of us since then.

That unity gave us strength to wait and withstand the pressures of fear, anxiety, and disappointment.

Most of these pressures, i.e. those relating to the divorce, were to last another three long years. But finally, I stood in my cell one day, going through my mail, when I came across a letter from the court. Somehow I knew what it was. I smiled to myself as I opened it. I grinned when I read it.

It was, of course, the letter which informed me that my divorce had been granted. It meant that Marilyn and I could finally be married. Other than my freedom, I can't think of anything that all of us had looked forward to more. But in a very real sense, this notification was merely putting in writing, what in practice, already existed. We (the seven of us) were already a family. But nonetheless, the divorce and the new marriage that it made possible, both represented real milestones in our journey as a family.

On August 27, 1992, Marilyn, her mother, her best friend, Tammy and my stepson Mike joined the chaplain and myself in the prison visiting room. These were the maximum number of people that I could have present, even for my wedding. My stepson was a busy young man that day. He was both my best man and the one who gave the bride, his new mother, away.

Soon after the wedding, all five of my children were allowed to come and visit me at once.

Finally, both spiritually and in every other sense we were one family.

Chapter 24

THE TOOTHLESS LIBERAL LIONS

In 1992, I and many other inmates watched with the rest of America as Clarence Thomas narrowly won Senate confirmation as a Justice of the Supreme Court of the United States.

The moment of greatest interest and even drama was, of course, when the roll call of the Senate members was taken. The exact outcome was in doubt until almost the end of the tallying.

But one of the great moments for me came earlier in the proceedings, when Thomas seemed to set the leadership of the Judiciary committee back on its collective ear. Thomas, a conservative, black Republican, accused the Democratic controlled committee of conducting a "high-tech lynching" against him because, Thomas forcefully claimed, the committee leadership perceived him as an "uppity nigger." Miraculously, Thomas's accusation stuck. The toothless liberal lions (Kennedy, Simon, Biden, et al.) just sat there and took it. Later they virtually apologized to Thomas on the way to assuring both him and the rest of the country that they had no such intention.

We convicts (most of whom were black) cheered Thomas on as he stuck it to his white, supposedly powerful inquisitors. Outside the realm of athletic competition, black men seldom get the better of white men in America and this was a rare treat for us to see.

The more sophisticated of us realized that it wasn't a matter of black versus white. We knew that it was a matter of party politics at the highest possible level—a conservative Republican president against the liberal Democratic leadership of the Senate. Some of us could see that it was a combination of Bush's muscle in the Senate, a conservative national tone, and waning liberal influence which decided the contest.

We tried to convince the other inmates of this as they stood there cheering Thomas on in the black versus white context. I think most of them really understood what the story was, but they kept cheering Thomas on anyway.

Not one of those toothless liberal lions had either the nerve or the knowledge of history to say that a black man has never been lynched in this country for anything that he might have done to a black woman (in this case, Anita Hill), sexual harassment, rape, murder, or otherwise.

Thomas won the point by default and went on to win the confirmation.

The liberals were unable to respond, in part, because they lacked the moral authority to even talk about the inappropriate behavior of another man in view of what one of them had recently revealed about his own behavior. Another reason why a strong response was not coming was simply that the day of the liberal had long since passed.

Earlier in the book, you may remember me praising John and Robert Kennedy. I didn't praise them because they were young and had great teeth—although that was certainly true. These were truly great men who died exposing the injustices of our time. Their lives continue to inspire American generations. Interestingly enough, it has been noted that the Kennedys themselves were actually a lot less liberal than many of those who have claimed that mantle since then. For instance, John Kennedy used the Cold War issue of a missile gap to defeat Richard Nixon in 1960. Yet Kennedy's commitment to human rights was indeed intact and impeccable.

Democrats love to talk about all the terrible things that came into being during the Nixon-Ford and Reagan-Bush eras, which up to 1992, encompassed twenty out of twenty-four years of white Republican domination. But before latter-day Democrats break their arms patting themselves on their backs for not being responsible for the ills of that era, they should look at the prison systems that they, the self-proclaimed political descendants of the Kennedys, have wrought.

Democrats must take ample blame for the terrible conditions found in American prisons today. This is partially because, other than the federal prison system, virtually all prisons are run by state governments. And Democrats have dominated state houses and state legislatures for most of the second half of the twentieth century. This is a period which certainly eclipses the often so-called twenty dark years of Nixon, Ford, Reagan, and Bush.

True enough, of the two major parties, the Democrats stood up for things which were in the best interest of both prisoners and society—such as more humane treatment and better educational opportunities and vocational training. The liberals among the Democrats also opposed the death penalty which the Supreme Court found unconstitutional in the seventies. But that is where their credit ends, and the long list of things which they must bear the blame for begins.

First of all, liberal Democrats opposed the construction of new prison facilities, largely on the grounds that they felt the money should have gone into crime prevention. This was an excellent cause and principal for which to fight. There was only one problem. Our Democratic friends forgot to do what politicians are supposed to do for the sakes of their constituents, principles, and their own political positions—they refused to compromise.

Because they refused to compromise, we the prisoners

got virtually no improvements and most of the prisons they had so vehemently opposed were built anyway.

The sad irony is that the Democrats painted themselves into a liberal corner, in which we, the inmates, are the ultimate and permanent prisoners. Politicians, whether Democratic, Republican, liberal, or conservative, come and go. We, the convicts, come and *stay*—not at the will of people like politicians but at the will and discretion of sentencing judges.

On the gubernatorial level, moderate Democratic governors have been elected in recent decades, so they must share some of the blame with the liberals.

On the federal level, Democrats are responsible for the fact that the federal prison system has deteriorated during the time that they have controlled both houses of congress. The control of both houses gave the Democrats the power to at least try to improve prison conditions in the federal system but they didn't take the opportunity.

And so as my fellow black convicts cheered on George Bush's black choice for the Supreme Court I watched with great interest and fascination. Never had I seen so many black men (and black men in prison at that) cheer *against* a Kennedy in my life. I knew the days of liberalism were truly gone.

All that was left were some memories and some toothless liberal lions.

Chapter 25

FATHERS BEHIND BARS

I had my children and my wife. I had a family. I was beginning to feel like a father. The scolding and the coddling, the laughter and the tears, the love and frustration made it real to me. Real and sad. I still didn't have my freedom. And after the last time that my appeal was denied, I fell into depression once more. The dreams of hanging myself started again. It was terrible.

I also began to dream a new dream, about the man I killed and how I killed him.

Over and over I saw his chest explode. I'll never forget the cloud of blue-gray smoke at the end of the shotgun, and the awful silence that followed the deafening blast. I saw his head snap back and his eyes roll back in what was the last moment of his life.

Then my dream would take me where I had never been, but to what must have happened in reality. I saw the man being embalmed, dressed for his funeral, rolled into a church, and then mourned by his family. I was there in the dream every step of the way to the man's grave. I could hear myself yelling: "Self Defense!... Self Defense!... The man was going to kill *me*... It was self defense!" But none of the mourners heard or noticed me. I joined a long line of people who filed past the man's coffin. I was at the very end of the line. When I finally reached the coffin, I looked down and saw the man in the coffin was my brother, Greg.

Of course, I had not killed my brother, but clearly my conscience was telling me I would never forget what I had done. Even though the killing was done in self defense, the man's death was as devastating to his family as Greg's death had been to me.

I concluded that I now had an even greater debt to repay than I had imagined. In addition to my sentence, I had to do something that would make life better for people other than my family. It was clearly a matter of conscience in terms of the torment I was going through, but there was more.

After thinking, praying, and talking with Marilyn, a picture began to develop. I had to do something to help others who were like me, and like the man I killed. These are men who are trapped in lives of crime, poverty, and prison. By doing this, I could morally as well as legally atone for what I had done.

But what to do? I had nothing to give, I thought. What little money I earned from my prison work was sent home to help support my children. Marilyn was now working literally night and day to support our five children and herself.

I sometimes lost track of how much and how hard Marilyn was working. This was because I never saw her come and go to work and because she rarely complained. She was carrying the financial and parental burdens of two people. I didn't have enough of anything for my own family, I realized. How could I seriously consider giving something to others?

Marilyn showed me the way. She explained that she would indeed continue to shoulder the family's financial responsibilities for as long as she had to. She also said that given my circumstances, the small amount of money

I was making and sending home was an important contribution that was genuinely needed and appreciated.

Marilyn also pointed me in the direction of this book, *Father Behind Bars*. She told me that I had lived an exceptional life and that others should know how I, or perhaps I should say we, lived, suffered, and survived. Marilyn also encouraged me to get more involved with activities in the prison, in addition to my writing for the paper. This led me to the many other outlets for my desire to make a contribution, one of them being the N.A.A.C.P.

Carl Meritt, Jr., the then president of the Kinross Michigan Chapter of the N.A.A.C.P. asked *me*, an inmate doing time for manslaughter, to become a member of one of the most distinguished and important human rights organizations that has ever existed. Carl didn't know it then but I was deeply moved and honored. The feeling increased when Carl asked me to chair the branch's Press and Publicity Committee. I was in charge of outside communications and the chapter's newsletter. The newsletter is entitled "ECHOES." It won the Thalheimers award in 1993 for "...it's dedication to, and the further improvement of, mankind."

From this point, I put together the Kincross prison's Black History Committee, which organized a multicultural Black History Month observance in 1993. It was the first program of its kind, that I had ever heard of, to be presented. When I was putting it together, I thought it would be useful to make the program something that would help to bring *all* the men in the prison together, not just isolate one group. So on the day of the program, Jews, Muslims, Irish, Italians, and every other ethnic group in the prison *joined* with African Americans to pay tribute to the contributions of black men and women in America.

I also began to feel that something had to be done to help the black family, particularly the families of convicts. This kind of help meant and means keeping those families together. Finally, there it was. I had thought of something that would help me *and* my brothers behind bars, too. It would be more than just a book that would simply tell my story, it would be a living and lasting instrument that could empower other men to create their own stories of success.

And so, after receiving enthusiastic approval and support from the prison authorities, I went to it. Once again the N.A.A.C.P. played a critical part in my efforts. The organization which is today called "Fathers Behind Bars" is at this time set up under the auspices of the N.A.A.C.P. chapter branch here at the prison. Our goals and objectives include: To help fathers in prison re-establish ties with their children and if possible the mothers of their children, to help these men become prepared for family life on the outside, and to give them the confidence and tools to start that process while they are still in prison.

We have really done well so far. We believe that we are giving men hope and the skills they need to be good fathers inside and outside of prison. Other than ourselves, there is no equipment, books, charts, guest speakers, or props—it's just us, confronting our failures and nurturing our potentials as men, and as fathers.

The convicts who have come into the group so far are varied in terms of their ethnic backgrounds and ages. But they are mostly black and mostly young. I am glad about this. Every man needs lessons in fatherhood and family leadership. But for young blacks, it is absolutely critical.

These sessions are intense.

I have seen men come into the group, grapple with issues of fatherhood, family, and personal responsibility just once and then never return. Not because of lack of interest, but because what they found in Fathers Behind Bars was very personal, very strong, and very painful.

But the fact that they felt pain means that they still have pride and sensitivity. And that means, if they build up their personal character and strength, they can still do it—they can still make it as fathers.

The news of Fathers Behind Bars spread, and I got letters from guys in other prisons asking about this concept of having men in prison reclaim and reunite with their families.

The requests for information regarding Fathers Behind Bars, and how to start new chapters in other prisons, got to the point that in addition to this book, the most efficient way to move things forward in this effort was to start a regular newspaper column headed with the organization's name.

Right now, the column is printed in many prison papers around the country. And like the hope I have in my heart, the hope that writing has given me, the momentum is building.

Chapter 26

A SONG FOR MY FATHER

I never sang for my father. Not once. And at the time of this writing, I don't know if my father is alive or dead.

But I do know that someday my children will want to know what he, their grandfather, was really like. They will want to know more than what I have written in this book, and I must find the answers to tell them. Before I can do this, I must reconcile. I must make peace with either his memory or his existence. I cannot be the father, or the leader of fathers, that I should be until I have become the son I should have been.

To simply relegate my father to being nothing but a drunk and an abusive person is too simple. He was and is more than that.

He was, after all, the man who married my mother, and the man who, with my mother, gave my siblings and I life. And in the early days of the family, we were happy and there was no abuse.

There was work for my father in those early days, he

was a different man. He was kind and often gentle. My mother told me that my father loved us all then and that he was our leader and protector. In those days, he *and* my mother drank, but they drank to socialize, to celebrate. But after my father's excesses my mother never drank again.

My father lost work because of his lack of education, skills, and youth. When he lost his work he lost his family. He, like many men, had no tools to deal with his own obsolescence. The ability to support his family was an inextricable part of his definition of being a father and a man.

No one counseled, retrained, outplaced, or took notice of my father as he shrank from being the leader of a family to being a piece of discarded rubbish on America's economic scrap heap.

A young man, untrained and uneducated without work is a shameful waste, but an old or aging, once productive, now idle, man represents the same sort of waste, and is even harder on the individual. If nothing else, the young man has the comfort of feeling that there is time to set things right, and that is the basis of all hope.

My father did not run out of time the way he often ran out of money. The money he ran out of was usually money he spent. The time he lost was taken from him before he had a chance to spend it or live it. It was taken from him in the profitable fashion of replacing able men with younger men.

What I want to say to you and sing to you, my father, is: Daddy, I understand how you lost your way and I love you. Age, education, and suffering has taught it to me. And this process has revealed to me the goodness of the man that my mother married.

You are now a man that I look up to and perhaps I always should have. Despite all your problems being out of work—like I was—being unable to support your family—like I was—despite your substance addiction, as far as I know, you were never arrested for any crime. In that respect you are a role model for your grandchildren, me and many others. I am also proud of your World War II heroics as a soldier for the U.S. Army.

The goodness that she hoped for each time she opened the door of reconciliation to you. And the goodness that just may have been in your heart whenever you walked through that door. The goodness that's been crushed by your suffering.

I pray that you are still alive Daddy. It would be fitting and wonderful if my arms and the arms of those in my family could embrace you lovingly the same way my understanding already has. My family wants to spend the rest of time with you. But the rest of our lives will have to do.

But if you are not alive Daddy, I will still live this life here on earth. Whether in or out of prison, I will try to live the kind of life that would have made you and Mama proud. With the love and strength of the wonderful family that I have I know I'll make it. Don't worry. I'll see you in heaven with Mama and Greg.

Soliloquy

The bitterness seeps forth,
and spreads like a foul wind.
How many more years?
How many more tears?
Lord, tell me;
how many more fears?

Oh! you cantankerous man
why must you complain?
Why must you snivel?
Tis' your bed you made.
Now you must lie,
now you must sleep,
all your troubles;
self inflicted, and now,
you dare to weep?

His hatred burns through steel,
porated to all against him.
Tension mounts, hopes subside,
more thoughts of self-infliction.
How many more years?
Lord, tell me...
How many more tears?

Oh you remonstrating fool,
you committed the crime,
now serve your time.
Stop thinking the world so cruel.

His love now showers many,
his bitterness abates,
the frustration no more,
to GOD he relates.

Oh you woe-be-gone man
with your fears no more,
you can live in peace
with yourself,
and the Lord.

A MESSAGE FROM THE PUBLISHER

W. R. Spence, M.D.
Publisher

Shortly after graduating from medical school in 1960, I spent two years in the U.S. Public Health Service as a physician assigned to a federal correctional penitentiary hospital. Little did I realize that 30 years later I would be publishing a steel-hard book, written by a convict, with a message for all America.

When William Banks and I first visited Arthur Hamilton at the penitentiary, Arthur's wife, Marilyn, and their five children agreed to come spend the weekend talking with us in the prison's visiting room. Halfway through our visit, I said to Banks, "This is a story of a father behind bars," and the title for the book was born.

At WRS Publishing, we are only interested in producing books we can be proud of—books that focus on people and/or issues that enlighten and inspire, books that change lives for the better, either through the celebration of human achievement or the revelation of human folly. **Call us at 1-800-299-3366 for suggestions or for a free book catalog.**

WATCH FOR THESE RELATED TITLES:

THE GHETTO SOLUTION, an intimate portrait of Roland Gilbert, how he overcame a life of self-inflicted pain, drug-addiction, and incarceration and went on to create **Simba,** a "rites-of-passage" program designed to teach African American men and boys to break the cycle of ghetto conditions.

CHAINS TO ROSES, the harrowing story of Joseph Cicippio's five-year ordeal as a hostage of Shiite Muslim kidnappers.

MAD MAN IN WACO, the complete story of the Branch Davidian Cult, David Koresh and the siege, as told by the world authorities on the Waco cult.

SURVIVING THE AGE OF FEAR, the story of Bill Langlois, San Francisco's heroic decoy cop who was mugged 256 times in the line of duty. It contains life-saving lessons from a leading expert on senior-citizen muggings.

WRS
PUBLISHING

A Division of WRS Group, Inc.
Waco, Texas